A LIFE WORT

A LIFE WORTH LIVING

THE 9 ESSENTIALS

BARRIE SANFORD GREIFF, M.D.

Previously published under the title *Legacy*

ReganBooks
An Imprint of HarperCollinsPublishers

A hardcover edition of this book was published under the title *Legacy* by ReganBooks, an imprint of HarperCollins Publishers, in 1999.

HarperCollins books may be purchased for educational, business, or sales promotional use. For information please write: Special Markets Department, HarperCollins Publishers Inc., 10 East 53rd Street, New York, NY 10022.

First paperback edition published 2001.

Library of Congress Cataloging-in-Publication Data has been applied for.

ISBN 0-06-098753-7

01 02 03 04 05 ❖/RRD 10 9 8 7 6 5 4 3 2 1

To my loving parents and special wife
Carole, and my insightful children and
awesome grandchildren.

We understood and believed in each
other, and that made all the difference.

If you are planning for the year, grow rice.
If you are planning for the decade, grow trees.
If you are planning for the centuries, grow
  men and women.

—*Chinese Proverb*

CONTENTS

ACKNOWLEDGMENTS

Herman Melville wrote that whaling ships were the Harvard and Yale of his life. My people, and the stories they have shared with me, have been my sailing vessels.

They have kept things afloat during times when the seas were turbulent. They have redirected me when my compass conked out. They have been the inspiration behind my managing to move forward, at times against heavy odds. I am deeply grateful for their friendship, wise guidance, and occasional kick in the butt when it was needed.

The stories in this book are real. In all cases I modified them to protect people's privacy. I have tried to the best of my ability to give credit to any work quoted. No one can write a book like this without leaning on—and drawing counsel from—the wisdom of giants.

The birth of a book is attended by many parents:

Helen Rees, my agent, had the foresight to understand what the book could be—and the talent to make it happen. Behind her funny, charming smile and compassionate nature exists a laserlike shrewdness that has totally captivated me.

Rick Manning helped shape the proposal for the book and helped edit the final manuscript. We caught each other at pivotal points in our lives. I admire his smarts, patience, and courage. His insights and sensitive antennae energized me. And he introduced me to ancient characters that I had only dimly known. Thanks for Gilgamesh.

Judith Regan at HarperCollins has the special quality of a great editor—the gift of elegant restraint. Thank you for understanding the tone of the book and capturing its message. Thanks also to Vanessa Stich for her calm and focused approach in shepherding the hidden necessities in creating a book.

A number of people have been my rock for many years. They are my "go to" people when I need help. We share a similar philosophy—that we must wear the scars of battle if we would wear the victor's crown.

They know who they are: Dan and Debbie Greiff, Ruth Carnat, Paul and Syrille Rosman, Barry Shiller and Michelle Julien, Cora Cohen, Duane and Kit Hagen, Charlie and Shirley Boren, Sonny and Maggie Katzenberg, Stan and Helaine Miller, Rob and Ronnie Bretholtz, Carol and Allen Wyett, Richard and Beverlee Brooks, Paula and Ralph Gilbert; my colleagues at the Harvard Business School, the Harvard University Health Services, Putnam Investments and Peabody & Arnold; Father James Gill, Rabbis Chiel, Warmflash, and Gardenswartz, the Krupp family, Gordon and Jennifer Silver, the Casty's, Richard and Jackie McCabe, the Frieze family, Sonny Gordon, the

Society of St. John the Evangelist, the Newton Public Library, the Temple Emanuel Library, the Portland, Maine Art Museum, and the art museum in Quebec City.

Jay and Patti Rohrlich, Charles and Andy, Ben Shapiro, Carl Sloan; the Lowensteins, Alrods, and Harrises; the Wolk family; Jonathan and Sam Isaacson, Linda and Steve Elmont, Randy Philips, Brian Babcock, George Berkowitz, the Winstons, Hap Porter, Barry Shragg, Ryan McCoughlin, Phillipe and Nanbe de Gaspe Baubien, Wayne Weiner, Dick McKinnon, Bruce Arons, Charles and Yvonne Goldsmith, Sara Delano, David Blau; Joan Leibovich, Eugene Freedman, Murray May, Rif Freedman, Charles Swearingen, Verne Harnish, the Perskys, the Green family, Sandy Levine, Richard and Beth Marcus, and Mel Rosenblatt.

There are many more, impossible to list. I thank you all for opening the doors of your companies and minds to me.

And finally, I would like to thank those who didn't get it. I took what you said to heart. In your own way you forced me to focus on what needed to be done, and to try again and again to get it right.

My challenge in writing this book was, to quote Samuel Johnson, "to lend courage to virtue and ardor to truth." And my friends and colleagues all helped me in that task.

PROLOGUE

I went to the woods, because I wanted to live deliberately, to front only the essential facts of life and see if I could learn what it had to teach and not, when I came to die, discover that I had not lived.

—Henry David Thoreau, *Walden*

When We All
Lived in the Forest

We find ourselves in the spring of our contentment: we've put a century of war and economic disruption behind us, and things appear to be going better than ever.

The domestic economy is booming, unemployment is down, interest rates are low, and mutual funds are bursting at the seams. People are buying more, and medical science has rewarded us with longer and healthier lives.

The world is at peace for the first time in three generations, and a century of war and tumult is coming to a close as we never could have expected it to, even ten years ago. Our collective sense of hope and optimism seems almost palpable as we approach the millennium.

Yet beneath this glossy veneer of hope, I have come to sense an uneasiness within the people I talk to and meet every day. Many seem to hear a still, small voice within themselves. Although they appear to be standing on terra firma, they feel a subtle shifting of underlying tectonic plates. It tugs at their sense of comfort and security.

This still, small voice constitutes more than a

remembrance of things past from a war- and depression-torn century about to close. Rather, it is a voice that speaks to us through centuries of human existence. And the voice says, essentially: "Hold on there, pal. One of these days the bread is going to land with the butter side facedown."

This voice, I think, has been with us since we all lived in the forest, an innate sixth sense that was probably best characterized by John Irving in his wonderful novel *The World According to Garp*. Irving called the foreboding "The Undertoad." Just as you figure things are going right, something will arrive to pull you down.

I'm convinced that this sense that "for everything there is a season . . . a time to plant and a time to harvest . . . a time to seek, and a time to lose" has allowed us, as humans, to survive as a species. This odd adaptive sense acts as a brake on our natural appetites, aspirations, and ambitions.

This sense kept us from following the wounded bear into the cave ten thousand years ago, knowing extreme danger—and bad odds—lay inside. This sense made us set aside one bushel of corn from every ten after we decided to put down roots and cultivate fields. We simply knew, instinctively, that the odds remained good that the following year would see no rain and no harvest and that we would need to dip into our treasure trove of reserves. And this same sense still keeps us from drawing to an inside straight because we know the odds of drawing the right card are just no good. So we keep the chips between our elbows and fold. We have survived because we know caution.

We survived because we maintain a quiet fright about the possibility of a major downturn—whether it's in the stock market today or the size of the wheat crop 3,500 years ago. Trees, we also came to understand, never grow to the sky, and everything has its limits.

Yet we also survived because some time ago we chose to search for a spiritual safety net that incorporated beliefs and values not subject to the whims of the marketplace or nature—beliefs that address not the times but the eternities, as Thoreau put it. The search is what makes us human, after all. We prepare, but not just as squirrels do for a coming winter. We humans prepare our souls and spirits for success and failure, renaissance and death, rain and drought, and hope and despair. Among those who started out in the forest, we alone retain this sense of mortality—this sense that our lives have meaning and value. And that living life well means more than merely surviving

And we remain the only ones with a sense of posterity as well. We alone harbor a concept in our souls that goes beyond protecting our young and those we love in the here and now. Bears and birds care for their young but we separate ourselves from the others in the forest in that we alone harbor something as ephemeral as the notion of passing something on to others after we pass on. This inclination is part of our innate sense that the odds will sooner or later turn, that "The Undertoad" will arrive on the scene, and that the time to harvest or die will eventually come.

Originally, when we all lived in the forest, we thought of posterity in terms of passing along nothing more than the spring's accumulation of berries, the fall's collection of acorns and nuts, and the summer's bountiful harvest from the fields and streams.

Yet as time passed and we became more removed from the forest, we began to think in terms of passing along more than mere material goods. We came to understand that there were more ways to protect the ones we love than by bestowing on them the means to hold off hunger and cold and want. We began to develop a sense that our stories, our experiences, our sense of what we'd learned, formed a protective armor every bit as worthy of passing on as the breastplate, shield, and plumed helmet. So in a very real sense the Bible, the *Iliad,* and other ancient texts were the first intellectual bequests—lessons, at first orally transmitted, to pass on to those who survived. They're epics—as are all of our lives — that involve a journey, a quest for values, a triumph of the sacred, and a homecoming. There's a reason that the epic form has lived for thousands of years. It's us.

Yet this tradition of the oral legacy—or call it the spiritual bequest—lapsed over time as we moved farther away from the forest. We came to see posterity almost exclusively in terms of material things.

Over the years, I have seen something in my work that leads me to believe that we humans yearn for a resurgence of these intellectual bequests. I attribute this to a kind of spiritual valence—the attraction we feel toward a specific belief—that makes us want to indicate how we as individuals should feel about values and situations. Many people I meet and talk with every day openly question whether we have become too "caught up in the thick of thin things" to the detriment of other, spiritual things. The joy/stuff ratio has its limits. "For what shall it profit a man if he should . . . gain the whole world and lose his soul," according to the New Testament. What a powerful message we've been given.

I sense a yearning in these people, a desire to pass on something more than the material wealth they have accumulated. They want to pass on something of themselves—something of the spirit—of who they are and what they have meant.

They seem to have come to an understanding, after asking "What is the measure of my worth?," that net worth means more than a simple bottom line. None of us wants to assess our life using merely the cold measure of the financial counting game. Net worth is the sum of three things: cash and securities, material objects, and spiritual values, or, if you like, spiritual capital. I like to think of net worth as an evenly balanced three-legged stool, the kind where you simply cannot identify the most important leg. Many seem to say, "My life has more relevance than simple economics after a lifetime of living and contribution. I refuse to be thought of as a balance sheet."

꧁ ꧂

My work helps me see this sense in people.

I have practiced as a psychiatrist in a number of unique settings for the last four decades; three years in residency training at the Institute of Living in Connecticut, one of the oldest psychiatric hospitals in the world; two years as a naval officer directing the Child and Adolescent Clinic at Bethesda Naval Hospital; two years at the Harvard University Health Services during the height of the counterculture, and sixteen years as the Psychiatrist to the Harvard Business School. For the past fourteen years I have remained as a consultant to the Harvard University Health Services and have conducted a practice in Cambridge, consulting to a host of Big Board companies, a mutual fund company, law and accounting firms, and family-held businesses.

In that time I have been privy to the inner workings of the minds of some of the brightest people in the world. I have worked with senior executives at large corporations grappling with an increasingly connected global economy. I have traveled to small towns, listening to workers trying to catch their breath as they defend their turf, fearful that "the only game in town" will be found obsolescent. An Alabama factory where four generations work together revealed to me lessons about the complicated relationships that exist between family and work that I could never have learned from a case study. I've worked with men and women of all ages and occupations attempting to make sense of their world turned upside down. All seek some kind of spiritual renaissance—some lodestar to guide them and connect them to certain immutable values that we have lived with, and by, for thousands of years.

To me the experience of working with these people

emerged as simple further proof that in large part we remain spiritual beings. Material wealth, no matter how much of it we earn, is a limited way to keep score. In the end, it takes a far second place behind our experiences in loving, learning, laboring, laughing and lamenting, leading, linking, living, an leaving a legacy.

And this realization led me to ask myself: if that's the case, then why, in exercising our innate sense of planning for posterity, do we no longer bequeath of our spirits? Why do we not bequeath what is most precious to us—not only what we have earned, but also what we have learned?

❧❧

Maybe it was a series of serendipitous events that led me to explore these ideas in a book, or a stream of coincidences that came together at the same time.

An associate who was a squash partner of twenty years was diagnosed with a serious illness. Another longtime friend was diagnosed with a brain tumor. At around the same time, someone gave me a book on "ethical wills," statements since the year 1050 drawn up by people and read after their deaths—expressions of moral and ethical values to transfer to the next generation. It was a volume that drew the distinction between extraordinary wealth and shallow benchmarks, and the wills took as their premise a sense that "Words that come from the heart enter the heart." That struck a chord in me.

Another friend gave me a moving volume he'd written and photographed on searching for beach glass north of Boston. These findings of his searches along the shore for brightly colored blues and greens and clears, in terms of a search for the host, the sacrament, were framed the ultimate wafer.

Maybe it was the passage of time, the loss of my parents, my own aging—and watching my wife and kids getting on—and the birth of my grandchildren that led me to embrace the idea of a living legacy and wrestle with it. Maybe it was something along the order of Abraham Lincoln who, when asked how long it took him to write the less than 280 words of the Gettysburg Address, replied, "All my life."

Yet despite that grandiose analogy, what I want to say, I say with humility. I've collected stories all my life, sharing with Isaac Bashevis Singer a belief that "stories are the memory of mankind." In doing so, I've tried to develop An Eye for an I—an ability to distill the essence of stories, knowing that what we receive from the past we can give to the future.

My profession does not give me a monopoly on knowing. In fact, I have learned more in the crucible of life through others than any textbook could possibly teach. And perhaps because of that, I'm left with an understanding and sense of awe that though we are all touched by the ocean, we all remain on the shore. No matter how much I know, or think I know, what I don't know remains far, far greater.

I know what I've seen and experienced. I also know how important the insights of others have been to me—and how often I've had to modify the beliefs and theories I held before I took advantage of those insights. The ancient Greeks understood that no one steps in the same stream twice, and that's more true now then it was in the Age of Heraclitus because we are more connected today and know that things change now faster than they did then.

But this is the best that I can offer as I stand by the shore, watching the waves of the unknown lap at the toes of my boots.

At this time of year I think of a living legacy of Moses carrying Joseph's bones out of Egypt and passing the leadership to Joshua, who enters the promised land—a kind of intergenerational baton exchange. At this time of year I think of Moses and Jesus and themes of freedom and rebirth, of overcoming adversity and creating hope, of failures and miracles, of the joining of evolution with revolution. I think of change and continuity and receiving and giving of memories and forgiveness. I think of how yesterday links with today and meets eventually with tomorrow. And that is what life is all about—finding the uniqueness in each and every one of us, celebrating that uniqueness, and preserving and sharing the legacy of special qualities that make human life worthwhile.

Passover/Easter Day
Spring 5759/A.D. 1999
Cambridge, Massachusetts

INTRODUCTION

Not "How did he die?" but "How did he live?"
Not "What did he gain?" but "What did he give?"
These are the units that measure the worth
Of a man as a man regardless of birth.
Not "What was his station?" but "Had he a
    heart?"
And "How did he play his God-given part?
    Was he ever ready with a word of good cheer,
    To bring back a smile, to banish a tear?"
Not "What was his shrine?" nor "What was his
    creed?"
But "Had he befriended those really in need?"
Not "What did the sketch in the newspaper say?"
But "How many were sorry when he passed
    away?"

> —*Anonymous*

WHEN DEATH
BECOMES LIFE

On a hot, steamy August day many years ago, my wife and children and I and were driving through the undulating hills of Vermont not far from Quichee Gorge.

We passed a farm sign that announced Asparagus For Sale. I stopped to buy some. Having grown up in Brooklyn, New York, I was curious about how the stuff grew.

I approached the farmer working in his field and started talking with him. He was in his mid-fifties, of medium build, and had a weather-beaten Vermont kind of look. But something about the farmer struck me immediately as odd. The two middle buttons of his long-sleeved denim shirt were undone, and I could see what appeared to be a baseball umpire's chest protector sticking through the opening between the folds of fabric.

Sensing our discomfort with the heat, the farmer invited us into the house for some iced tea. We sat around his kitchen table in the center of the cool room, surrounded by all sorts of lumber and tools, which were strewn about in a haphazard way.

He asked what I did, and I said I was a physician. Without missing a beat, the farmer said matter-of-factly, "Oh, then you'd be interested to know that I'm dying."

His directness, as well as the gravity of the message, caught me off balance.

He went on to explain how he'd been practicing dentistry in California for a number of years, but how during the past year, he'd begun to feel tired and weak and that his bones had begun to hurt. He went to his doctor and discovered he had multiple myeloma, a disease that affects certain bones and makes them fragile and subject to fractures. He told me his prognosis was poor. His doctors didn't hold out much hope for recovery.

He went on to recount how he'd become depressed. "I wasn't prepared to leave life so early—especially when I felt there was so much to do," he said.

He sold his dental practice in California and returned to Vermont, which had been his home before he moved to the West Coast. He bought the nineteenth-century farmhouse we were sitting in and began to restore it. He stocked his pond with fish and planted an extensive vegetable garden. He seeded trees, which, he explained, would make their appearance in the years to come.

"I made a conscious, deliberate decision," the dentist-turned-farmer added slowly, "that as I die I would give life to everything around me. Those acts would define my existence."

I was deeply moved by what he said that afternoon

in the cool of his kitchen, and he continued to occupy my thoughts throughout the ensuing year. I couldn't help but be touched by his remarkable courage and vision—and by his strong need to leave a mark on the world even as he planned for his own departure.

The following summer we went back to the farm.

The repairs on the house had stopped. The hay fields hadn't seen a thresher and baler in months. The fields lay empty, practically void of vegetables. All that remained was the asparagus, which, he had explained to me the summer before, would take two seasons to grow from seed time to harvest.

A daughter or niece—I didn't feel it was my place to ask—told us the farmer had died in the spring. His disease had overcome him slowly. But he had died where he had chosen to die.

Saddened, I scanned the fertile fields, the trees, the life he had planted all around him. Even as he died, his message was abundantly clear. His loss would be a gain for others. One man had provided for generations to come. It brought to my mind the old saying, "The best fertilizer for a garden is the farmer's shadow."

Faced with the inevitable loss of his own life, he chose to survive in the true sense of the Latin word *supervivere*—to over-live: to live beyond his life, leaving an indelible signature on nature's canvas around him from which his survivors could benefit.

Friedrich Nietzsche said that "One who has a 'Why' to live, can deal with almost any 'How.'" I'd amend that to say that one who has a "Why" and a

"How" to live—and passes them on—can live forever.

When we encounter touchstone events that force us to use our inward eye, we ask powerful questions. All too often, those may be the only times we ask those important questions of ourselves. They may be the few times we do a personal accounting.

The farmer, it seemed to me, had decided not to accept the standard paradigm of death being the final end to life. Instead, he chose to turn closure into openings. He left a message that said we can convert despair into hope, loss into gain, and simple acts into sacred deeds. Decay can turn into growth, and uncertainties can turn into possibilities. He reminded me of something that Jacob Bronowski had written in *The Ascent of Man*: "Man is a singular creature. He has a set of gifts which make him unique among the animals. So unlike them, he is not a figure in the landscape. He is a shaper of the landscape . . . the ubiquitous animal who did not find but made his home in every continent."

The farmer shaped his decision to leave something behind that transcended his own here and now. His bequest for the future in a sense shrouded him with a touch of immortality—far more than any material goods he may have left behind. He made the heroic choice, borrowing a concept from Eastern philosophy, *jai bhagwin*. It means to salute the light within oneself—and illuminate everything around one for generations to come.

I've met many people like the farmer in the course of my work, and I've found that eight themes play themselves over and over again in the music of people's lives. As Thomas Cahill put it, "In a fundamental, ineradicable way, we still see with the eyes of our earliest ancestors, and our hearts still quicken to the same things theirs did."

At the end of the day, we need to pass on to our inheritors an understanding of these eight themes. They represent the light within ourselves that will provide illumination for generations that follow. They make up our sense of hope—our spiritual DNA for posterity. Our living legacy.

The first of these universal themes is the need to *Love*—to feel good about oneself and share love with special people. The second is the need to *Learn*—to explore, stretch and grow so as to adapt to novel situations. The third is to *Labor*—to create meaning and value in the work we do every day.

We need to recognize and experience a range of emotions in the course of living. To *Laugh* and experience the joy and pleasure of life. And *Lament* as we are humbled by the unfair and overwhelmed by the evil. We need to *Link* and create a number of sustaining connections with others in weaving the tapestries of our lives.

We need to *Live* and appreciate the cycles of life as the cycles revolve around us and we around them. We also as humans feel the urge to *Lead* and take risks, for that is much of what defines us. And we also learn to *Leave* and deal with disappointment and loss, which is around us every day.

In as much as one can generalize about matters of

this scope, those Eight L's make up the core of the human experience. Collectively, they are the ninth *L*—our *Legacy*. Loving, Learning, Laboring, Laughing and Lamenting, Linking, Leading, and Leaving. Cut through all the clutter and those eight themes represent our commonality—and our common gift to posterity.

They are the indispensable psychological building blocks that give us purpose, meaning, and vitality in dealing with the uncertainties and paradoxes inherent in an involved life. They are the "necessaries" for everyone regardless of income or social status. They apply to the king and the knave, the strong and the weak, the confident and the confused. They transcend religious and cultural beliefs. They will be as important in the future as they have been in the past—if not more so. They may appear separate but in reality they stand connected and feed off each other.

They are the "essential facts of life" that Thoreau set out in search of, and the "rock" that the Gospel of Matthew referred to: "And the rain descended and the floods came and the wind blew upon the house and it fell not for it was founded on a rock."

What's remarkable is not so much that we share these themes but rather that the themes remain constant even as we play out infinite variations on them individually. Bell ringers at the National Cathedral in Washington, D.C., ring the same eight bells for three-and-a-half hours and never hit the same combination twice—except for the simple scales at the very beginning and the very end of their peal.

These timeless truths, in other words, are always the same, but the applications differ from generation to generation. You can find the same message on a cuneiform tablet as on a piece of thermographic fax paper. The message is the same, but the form, context, and content are different.

This story may be apocryphal but it makes the point well. When Einstein was teaching at Princeton, he passed out a final exam to his gifted students. As the students worked on their solutions, Einstein's young teaching assistant became progressively more anxious and agitated. "Professor," he said to Einstein. "I think you've made a terrible mistake. The questions you asked this year are the same ones you asked last year!"

Einstein looked at his young assistant. In a measured, knowing voice, he replied, "You're correct. But there is no mistake. The questions are indeed the same this year as last year. Except this year, the answers are different."

Our imperfections—our different answers—give us our uniqueness and character. No one's life is ever complete, and no one can fill in all the spaces on the "exam form" of life. In Michelangelo's painting on the ceiling of the Sistine Chapel, the finger of God approaches—but does not touch—the finger of Adam. That means we never fully achieve what we set out to do—always needing more time to add the finishing touch, always stretching and always just approximating our goal.

Navajo artisans, in fact, deliberately weave a flaw somewhere into their tapestries: a tacit acknowledgment that only the gods are perfect and that we—and the tapestries of our lives—are not. One may be great at Loving and Laboring and only so-so at Learning. It matters not. Only the gods are perfect. We are what we are.

To a large degree, the Eight L's, which comprise our common legacy, have lost their focus and significance in our modern world. The ancients and poets seemed to understand the Eight L's as Legacy. We do not. Deceived by the allure and pace of modern lifestyles, we have lost an appreciation of them.

Tennyson imagined an aged and cranky Ulysses sitting on his throne at the end of his life, lamenting, as the Rolling Stones later sang, "What a drag it is getting old." ("How dull it is to pause, to make an end.")

Yet the old adventurer takes comfort in the fullness of his life and in the fact that ". . . all times have I enjoy'd/Greatly, have suffered greatly, both with those that/Loved me, and alone . . . I am a part of all that I have met."

That which we are, we are, Ulysses went on to say, and we never stop learning and experiencing life for as long as we live. He recognized that, and so did the dentist in Vermont. We owe it to life to continue living long after our hearts stop beating. We owe it to life to pass on our lives—and our lessons—to the untraveled world.

And we have to learn to live life with an appreciation of time. We can't be arrogant and assume that time waits for us when we are ready to use it. Time is a non-renewable resource, evanescent and irretrievable. To realize the value of a month, ask a mother who has given birth to a premature baby. To realize the value of an hour, ask two lovers who are waiting to meet. To realize the value of a second, ask a person who has survived an accident. To realize the value of a millisecond, ask an Olympic silver medalist.

A successful businessman who worked around the clock came to see me with his irate wife. She had begged him to go to any *one* of his son's basketball games during his senior year, but he had never been able to find the time. He had missed all of them, he admitted, but he had calculated one last date.

"There'll be time to see a game in the future," he said. "I'll plan my time better. This time it's going to be different. In fact, here, look at this, I've set aside the time next week," he added, showing his wife his Filofax.

She gave him a dark, menacing look and said slowly and deliberately, pausing between each word: "His . . . last . . . game . . . was . . . a . . . week . . . ago."

He sat in my office. We all felt the vibration of fifteen seconds of palpable silence. And then he put his head in his lap and began to sob uncontrollably for ten solid minutes. It was too late. He would never get a chance to see his son compete in a varsity game. He had missed the last one.

I felt deeply for the man as the tears streamed down his cheeks and came to rest damply on his white shirt collar. But I could not help thinking that he sends a lesson to all of us. It's not just that the next generation is precious and that we must pay them heed. Some things cannot be relived; we cannot control the calendar; we need to grab our special moments, because excuses will come back to haunt us.

We must also take the time here and now to consider our legacies, consider what we hold most important, and tell them to the next generation. Otherwise we as a people will carry forever the scars of regret far deeper than the tracks of the tears that etched themselves into that poor man's face. "'Tis not too late to seek a newer world," as the aging Ulysses said.

Poets, physicians, welders, and rock stars all share a common thread. We all do.

Jimmy Buffet wrote in his memoir, *A Pirate Looks at 50*:

In preparation for my 50th birthday, I went back to the cedar-lined steamer trunk in my basement in Long Island, where I store a considerable collection of notebooks, cocktail napkins, mildewed memo pads, and sparsely filled binders. These are the stories that have made up my songs and my life and I go back to them from time to time for ideas. What I know for sure is that there are a lot of smart middle-aged people, but not many wise ones. That comes with "time on the water" as fishermen say. We could all use a few more minutes out there.

We all have spent our time on the water. We all have cedar-lined steamer trunks, literal or figurative, in the basements of our homes or in the attics of our memories. And we all will spend more time on the water as our lives go on, and we continue to gather, if not wisdom, then experience at least.

We need to periodically open up those trunks and take out the mildewed notebooks and tattered cocktail napkins that bear the memories of lives well spent. They are gifts we've received from the past that we can then give to the future.

We need to record those stories that define for us Loving, Learning, Laboring, Laughing and Lamenting, Linking, Living, Leading, and Leaving. These have been our hope in the past; they are our hope for the future, and our chance to give life, meaning, and vitality to generations that follow us.

1

LEGACY

Be as a stone cast upon the water, that the positive influence of your action may extend far beyond the power of a mere pebble in the hand of a man.

—*Ancient Saying*

HONOR THY FATHER
AND MOTHER: WHY?

It was late in the afternoon, and we had just finished a company board meeting. A publicly traded division of the company had been sold, and the group toasted the occasion. As a result of the transaction, the two founders both came away with enough cash to finance a king's ransom.

One of the founders and I walked down Boston's fashionable Newbury Street, and a charming peace seemed to hang over that part of the city's Back Bay. Yet as we walked, and decided to take two seats at an outdoor cafe, my friend seemed curiously subdued.

I congratulated him on his windfall as our drinks arrived and offered another toast. He smiled and for a brief moment reflected on his achievement. But then from out of the blue he blurted: "What am I going to leave to my kids?" Briefly, he told me what I already knew—how he and his partner had worked their buns off to build the business, spending enormous amounts of time at the office and on the road, taking tremendous risks and overcoming some pretty hairy times in the market.

His thoughts as he talked about his kids strayed far from triumph, though. He acknowledged that they would be secure now. They would never have to work if they didn't want to, and they would have all the money they would ever need. But my friend was wise enough to appreciate the multiple faces of security.

His concerns, he explained, centered around his kids' sense of self-worth.

Financial armor alone did not protect anyone from the world, he said. Could they make a contribution to society that they would initiate themselves? Would his success—and their newfound wealth—take away their hunger, their enthusiasm, and their passion? Had he—through his own success—stripped his children of the pleasure of achieving something on their own? What kind of an impact would that have on their own senses of self-worth?

Clearly my friend wanted to act as someone who would be more than a "bottom-line" father. In a way, his financial success had crystallized the problem in his quick and active mind: how to pass on values more important than a king's ransom? How to pass on a spiritual cushion infinitely more valuable than his wealth?

In his own way, he highlighted the problem challenging the current generation that will transfer over seven trillion dollars worth of assets to their heirs— the largest amount of wealth ever passed from one generation to another in the history of the world.

I had heard these concerns many times before

from successful people. Each time I heard them, I recalled the words of Ralph Waldo Emerson: "What lies behind us and what lies before us are tiny matters compared to what lies within us."

My friend knew intuitively that we leave more than money and material objects to the next generation. We leave the best of ourselves. He knew his job was to reveal the best of himself to his children—and to make sure they knew he was passing that on as the most valuable legacy he could ever leave. Only in that way would the qualities of curiosity and hunger, passion and enthusiasm, risk and reward, disappointment and achievement, be passed down as a legacy to the generation he wanted to receive them.

Thinking of a legacy in its full meaning is the equivalent of moving from a finite analog world to an infinite digital one, from limited options to multidimensional ones, with more leverage and greater flexibility, with more meaning and a lot more clout.

I remember a while ago talking on the phone with my aging parents. At the time they lived fifteen hundred miles away in Florida, and communicating with them was difficult.

Their collective sense of judgment seemed badly impaired. My father carried large sums of money and displayed wads of bills in public; they mixed up each other's doctors' appointments; they made airplane reservations and then forgot about them; they decided to save money by not having the failing brakes on their car inspected. They had always been incredibly close, and their newfound eccentricities only received affirmation from each other. They lived in a self-contained world of their own. And it was a mess.

It's not easy watching the decline of loved ones, especially from a distance—and especially when they had once been extraordinarily competent and had passed on their guidance, wisdom, patience, and caring to me.

I was worried. I suggested some simple solutions. They agreed enthusiastically—and then proceeded to follow through on absolutely none of them. Their minds, once like Rolls-Royces, had lost four spark plugs and two quarts of oil, and their lives were sputtering along to a dead halt.

Life was becoming very difficult for them. And for me.

Because we were far apart and I could not monitor the situation, I became increasingly concerned, frustrated, angry, and resentful. I could sense impending disaster. As I was dealing with my sense of helplessness, the Old Testament commandment "Honor thy father and mother" jumped into my mind, and I asked myself for a brief insensitive moment, "Why should I honor them? They're making a complete mess out of everything. And they refuse to listen to reason."

I was angry at them, but then also suddenly angry and embarrassed at myself, at my arrogance for allowing the thought of abandoning them to enter my mind—especially when their defenses were impaired and they needed me. I was thinking only of myself, of my sense of magic at healing, and here it was being taken away from me.

So I did what I often do when I'm frustrated. Experience has taught me that a question may be an answer in disguise. The answer to my question about honoring my parents became instantly clear to me one night after hanging up from a typically frustrating conversation with them.

I honor them because they are my parents, because they were always there for me. They rarely judged me harshly and always supported my interests, even when those interests ran contrary to their own. And I honor them for that, too.

I honor them because they needed me, and it really didn't matter whether they followed through on the advice I was giving them. I honor them because they are the man and woman in me. To give that up would be to give up myself, literally.

And I honor them for the legacy they had passed on to me—all their wisdom, patience, compassion, and teachings.

At a later time, I learned that the Latin word for *honor* is the same as the word for *heaviness, weight, difficulty,* and *burden.* And the Romans were right. There is a certain amount of heavy lifting involved in maintaining honor and observing it on a daily basis— especially when the tide turns against you. And in the case of my mother and father, yes, the burden was heavy. The legacy, and the honor in it, became, in fact, a kind of unconscious reciprocal pact that we had drawn up between us. They took care of me and gave me gifts; I took care of them and gave them gifts in return. The honor part of a legacy inscribes a wonderful circle of life and shows the power of reciprocity.

And if we are able to absorb legacies simply by being around other people and distilling their messages, wouldn't our own legacies become that much richer if we passed on specific stories about Loving, Learning, Laboring, Laughing and Lamenting, Linking, Living, Leading, and Leaving?

The legacy we build and leave revolves around a central belief that our lives have stood for something—that we've been asked tough questions and somehow managed to survive, and in many cases, thrive. As Abraham Heschel said, "To be human is a problem"—and we define our humanness by how we handle our problems.

We are who we are not just by chance. We are connected to those who came before us, and in that very real sense we are keepers of their legacies, caretakers. We take the lessons we've learned from our parents, teachers and mentors and hold them close—because they give us comfort and courage, because we've learned from them, because we find they guide us well in our lives.

But we are not the owners of those lessons and legacies. They were given to us in trust to pass along. Ultimately, it's not what we own but what we share that makes a difference and that ties us to others, past and future. While some leave vast sums of money and property to their heirs, others, less affluent, have little to leave save memories, values, traditions, and stories that are far more valuable to their descendants than material goods. We all leave the earth eventually, but we never die to those who love and remember us well.

And the key to being well remembered? Sharing the stories that point out the values. Sharing the stories that point out the traditions we hold close and dear. Sharing the memories that bring comfort when the soul needs a soft caress on a cold winter night.

These stories are great gifts. As Saul Bellow has pointed out, a writer doesn't find a story; the story finds the writer. We have the power to take the stories that found us and bring them to our children—stories that demonstrate shades of openness and opaqueness, indifference and caring, cruelty and compassion, humbleness and arrogance, reciprocity and selfishness.

***

Three stories come to mind about passing on legacies. The first involves transforming a vow into an action.

A man I know has shown remarkable devotion and dedication in taking care of his wife, who has suffered from a severe neurological disorder for the past twenty years. He dresses and assists her in virtually every basic bodily function. He lifts her in and out of his car. He worries about her while he's at work. And he worries about himself and whether he will physically be able to continue assisting her.

At times he has felt he was losing out on life. Yet he has been able to deal with his own anger and lack of freedom. At the same time he has also found that he has harbored incredible feelings of admiration for her. He is amazed by her inner courage. Her ability to go to the well of personal strength and tenaciously fight back has engendered in him great feelings of tenderness.

He takes his wife scuba diving in the warm waters of the Caribbean, knowing the weightlessness and sense of freedom and mobility delight her. He throws a wonderful party at their house every spring as a way of celebrating the continuation of life, and several dozen close friends start looking forward to the party beginning around Easter and Passover time.

He said to me once, "I've been awed by her need to do things, to be part of the scene, and to be included in the lives of our friends and not capitulate. The litany of losses is all too easy to chronicle, but some of the wins are equally as great."

And he knew that he and his wife's strong relationship had left an important legacy to their two sons, aged twenty-four and nineteen.

"I see two men who have learned some very tough lessons," he wrote to me. "Both are sensitive to the needs of the disabled. Both have developed an empathy, a tenderness, and a strength to deal with loss and have understood the word *We* and not *I* in the family context. That will serve them well. They have been part of a family that has dealt with adversity and not buckled under. What more precious lesson could I offer them than the gifts of roots and wings?" The boys will carry their parents' legacy with them forever—all of what they were shown firsthand when the words "in sickness and in health, for better, for worse" were turned into reality.

The second story is a legacy of trust.

A man who grew up in the 1940s remembers the cedar closet by the front door, and even today, every time he smells the rich red scent of cedar, it always reminds him of a legacy from his youth.

His father kept a coat hanging on the same hook in the closet, and the pockets of the coat bulged with pennies, nickels, dimes, and quarters. Every night when his father came home from work, he would simply empty the change from his trouser pockets and drop the coins into the pockets of the coat in the cedar closet.

When the boy would come to his father for money for a treat or a movie, his father would always say, "Go to my jacket in the closet and take what you need." And the boy did—never a penny more—remembering well into his adulthood the lesson of trust, which smells in his mind even today of red cedar.

And then there is a story where the legacy is "Handle with Care."

A young man recalled his father, and a seemingly incongruous metaphor. "I drive," the father said, "in such a way that I try to never have another driver alter either his course or his speed solely as a result of something I do."

The son had once driven race cars for a living—he was now an administrator at a large professional firm—and saw instantly that the father was giving him an oral legacy.

His mother was ill, hopelessly so, and had been that way for some time. Why, the son had asked his father that night, should the father remain faithful to her? Why should he not strike out for comfort and succor in another direction? Why not look for something for himself?

The son immediately understood the father's metaphor for what it was: that we should act in life in such a way that nobody would be needlessly hurt or demeaned as a result of something we do. Further, we have to use our brakes to show restraint, our horns to sound alarms when we ask for help, to steer straight so as to stay out of the gutter, and to keep up a regular maintenance program to avoid sudden breakdowns.

A colleague mentioned to me a story she had heard on National Public Radio. A man had recently concluded a study of gravestone markings in cemeteries around New England. His odd, if revealing, finding: In the seventeenth, eighteenth, and nineteenth centuries, the vast preponderance of the grave markings related to character: that the interred had been a loving father, a devoted mother, a brave man, a courageous woman. The epitaph of Col. John Buttrick, who led the colonial militia at the battle of Concord on April 19, 1775, is a wonderful example: "Having laid down the sword with honor, he resumed the plough with industry, by the latter to maintain what the former had won."

In the twentieth century the vast preponderance of the inscriptions mention not character but profession. Yet character is what defines us—and character is what a legacy should be about. As the poet Horace wrote in 23 B.C., "I have erected a monument more lasting than bronze/And taller than the regal peak of the Pyramids./I shall never completely die."

We build our legacy every day. We leave character behind—our stories—shaped by a lifetime full of Loving, Learning, Laboring, Laughing and Lamenting, Linking, Living, Leading, and Leaving.

First among them is Loving.

2

LOVING

When you get what you want in your struggle
    for self
And the world makes you king for a day,
Just go to a mirror and look at yourself,
And see what that man has to say.
For it isn't your parents, your children or wife
Whose judgment upon you must pass.
The fellow whose verdict counts most in your
    life
Is the one staring back from the glass.
He's the fellow to please, never mind all the
    rest
For he's with you clear up to the end.
And you've passed your most difficult,
    dangerous test
If the man in the glass is your friend.
You may fool the whole world down the
    pathway of life
And get pats on the back as you pass.
But your final reward will be heartaches and
    tears
If you've cheated the man in the glass.

                              —*Anonymous*

"How Long Does a Hug Last?"

Whenever I get down and question my worth, I think of the parable of Joshua.

Joshua is a man in his early forties who looks around the community, compares himself to a number of people, and finds himself desperately wanting.

He feels he's not as smart as the professor next door or as rich as the entrepreneur down the street. Nor is he gifted as a great athlete, and he knows he will never be a Darwin or a da Vinci or a Galileo. "All I am is an ordinary man, nothing special," he says to himself, sadly.

Heavily burdened by these disappointments, he goes to bed one night and has a dream: God looks at him and asks a simple question:

"Joshua," says God, "You worry too much about not being like your neighbors, about not being brilliant like a Darwin or creative like a da Vinci or earth-shaking like a Galileo. Tell me Joshua, why weren't you like Joshua in your life?"

He awakens quickly, heart racing, full of fear. All of a sudden he understands the power of the question and feels an enormous sense of relief. He realizes that his task in life is not to mirror someone else's life but to be himself.

And then he realizes something even more powerful. In the history of the world there has been only one Joshua, even as there has been only one Darwin, one da Vinci, and one Galileo. And not even that awesome trio could be a Joshua.

Self-love remains the cornerstone of our ability to trust what we think and feel and do. It is the spiritual epoxy holding us together. It is the necessary ingredient in developing confidence in ourselves. It allows us to derive pleasure from our activities and gives us the courage to take risks. With it, we develop the guts to think out of the box and grow, viewing the world as an evolving, diverse, and connected series of events.

Self-love gives us the heart to hear the word *no* and not feel annihilated—and to accept *no* as a negotiable word. It helps us look at the future and see it in proper perspective. To paraphrase Victor Hugo, "The future has many names. For the weak it is the impossible. For the faint hearted, it is the unknown. For the thoughtful and the valiant, it is hope." Self-love opens us to hope.

If you don't believe in yourself, who will believe in you? If you don't respect yourself, can you have any reason to expect a different reaction from someone else? And if you don't think loving yourself in the broadest sense of the word is important, then how can you possibly accomplish what you're capable of achieving? We need to pass on to our children the importance of this sense of loving, respecting, and forgiving oneself.

—◦⟨⟩◦—

It was mid-March, and an icy snow fell outside my office in Cambridge. All day long. As the day wore on, I started to dread making the commute home. I knew all the roads would be icy and treacherous and the ride would be a long and miserable one.

My last appointment of the day was with a college student, a young man named Steven who had a powerful, charismatic father. He felt totally inadequate in his father's presence, and as a result, his sense of self-worth was very low. He was convinced he could never really do anything well—or certainly not well enough to measure up to the magnitude of his father's accomplishments. We had been working together for several months, yet had failed to make much real progress.

As we finished our session, I looked out at the falling ice, thought of the dreaded ride home, and remembered that Steven lived in the general direction of my house. I offered him a lift back to his dorm. He seemed surprised—as though therapists weren't supposed to offer patients rides home through ice storms—but he accepted my offer. I told him every rule had an exception, under the right circumstances, and that besides, I might need him to pull me out of a snowdrift.

We drove onto the entrance ramp to the Massachusetts Turnpike, and as we approached the exact-change toll booth, I threw a quarter at the basket. For the first time I could remember, I missed the mark. The coin dropped to the ground. Or more accurately, the quarter fell into a frozen soup of dirty slush.

I didn't have any additional change, and neither did Steven. So I got out of the car and began searching for the buried quarter in the slush. Here it was, six-thirty at night; dark and shadows and blinding headlights danced everywhere; and I couldn't find the coin. My game of find-the-quarter, meanwhile, had caused a major traffic backup, and every licensed driver in the Commonwealth, it seemed, was blowing his horn at me. It was every commuter's nightmare come to life.

After a couple of minutes of searching, I finally found the quarter and dropped it deliberately into the basket.

I tried to make light of my ineptitude as we drove away, but Steven did not respond at all, and we finished the ride to his dorm in silence.

I did not see Steven for several weeks. He arrived at my office for his next appointment on time and then proceeded to say nothing for the first 15 minutes. "You're very quiet," I remarked.

"Look," he said. "I was recommended to you because of your reputation. But driving home with you was one of the worst experiences of my life. As I watched you looking for that quarter, groveling in the snow, you looked so lost and helpless. And I couldn't bear it. I felt angry, embarrassed, and humiliated that the person I was seeing, the one who I relied on so much, appeared so totally incompetent." Then the tears welled up in his eyes. "You looked like I feel in relation to my father." He paused. "Helpless and incompetent." Tears streamed down his cheeks as his body shook with sobs.

That experience became a turning point in our work together. He could learn to deal with me as a human being, a collection of successes and failures. I was no longer an icon; nor was I a total bum: just a regular human being with frailties. He knew I had experienced pain—and certainly humiliation, because he had seen it—and he now knew that I could identify with and feel his pain.

We were able to make substantial progress on his issues of self-love. He came to see that he was not at all destined to be unworthy throughout his entire life just because he did not measure up to the stringent expectations of one person, with very different standards from his own. There was plenty to love about himself, and he came to understand that over time.

His legacy, which he can now pass on to others, is that one hole in the hull doesn't necessarily sink the whole boat, and that we are continually works in progress.

That message alone is vital to a living legacy.

<hr/>

Perhaps the story is apocryphal, but it makes its point well.

Oliver Wendell Holmes was once invited to address a group of illuminati. He was told that the topic could be anything he chose. He started his talk with the following:

"Thank you for the opportunity to address the group. Originally I thought I would talk about the world. But the subject seemed too narrow, so, instead, I'd like to talk about myself." Holmes clearly had some problems in his life, but a lack of self-love certainly was not one of them (at least not on the surface).

People with self-love have the common element of a genuine "realness," which makes them tolerable and approachable. They have their doubts and sometimes are insensitive. They mess up but don't dwell on their mistakes. They figure out ways to recover. They have the capacity to forgive themselves. They are far from Eagle Scouts and share the embarrassing and painful moments common to us all. But they also have perspective, a sense of contrition and knowledge that "I'm not as good as I think I am, but I'm also not as bad as I think I am."

They remain open to fresh ideas without feeling manipulated or stupid because they didn't think of the new idea first. And when they're criticized they don't take a single correction as a blanket indictment of their overall abilities. They try not to abuse themselves or allow others to abuse them. They have pride, and they're not afraid to take a position and be challenged by others.

For example, I learned of a father who successfully ran a retail store for a number of years. He'd inherited the business from his father and planned to pass the store on to his son after he got his MBA.

But it was never to be. The father continued to run the business, and the son poked his head in periodically to offer suggestions on how to streamline the operation and make it more efficient.

In fact, the son was shocked at how primitive the "systems" were: a scrap of paper here and there, some numbers attached to a name, indicating partial payment. It looked like total chaos.

He gently approached his father. "Nothing has an order to it," he said. "How do you know if you're making any money or not?"

"When I started in the business, I had one shirt," he said to his son, readily conceding that his book-keeping methods did not square with general accounting practices. "But we now have two beautiful homes and a couple of cars. We have money in the bank and a substantial number of securities. And we have no debt. So by my calculations, if you take all our assets and subtract the one shirt, we're way ahead of the game."

People with self-love are like that.

Self-love also carries with it the ability to develop a sense of "unlonely aloneness." This is the quality of valuing and benefiting from solitude—and being charged by it. Those with self-love trust their instincts, in part because they have been exposed to unexpected events and survived intact.

People with self-love know how to joint-venture because they trust selectively and take risks. Because they believe that if you don't shoot, you don't score, they also know that when you do shoot, you don't score every time.

They have faith in their decisions based on clear values that are not subject to the whims of the marketplace. And they accept their vulnerability—not as a sign of weakness or dependency but as an opportunity to grow and learn. A mother once asked her ten-year-old son if he'd packed everything for his first sleep-away camp. "Yes," he replied. "Everything except my courage."

They are able to deal with alienating, uncomfortable thoughts or feelings because they understand that in the theater of the mind, all kinds of bizarre activities take place. And they have the heart to care, to see where the pain is.

No one permanently owns the concept of self-love. It is not a fixed or immutable commodity like corn or platinum. The most assured people can lose their confidence in a fraction of a second like morning haze burning off under the heat of the August sun. Holding on to self-love requires risk and courage over a lifetime with many obstacles and detours as we make our way through the labyrinth of life.

What is *The Wizard of Oz* about? It's a story about a tornado, yes, and a wicked witch, yes, and about the Yellow Brick Road. And it's a tale about four companions searching for the Emerald City and the Wizard. You could just as easily say that *Moby Dick* is a just a book about whaling.

The Wizard is actually a story about four people in search of self-love.

Dorothy, in a foreign land, frightened and disconnected, longs to return home. She meets three characters, each with a major deficiency. The four of them go looking for transplants to make them whole. The Scarecrow has no brain. The Tin Man has no heart. The Lion has no courage, and Dorothy has no home. Between them, they lack smarts, feelings, guts, and a comfort zone. Not my ideal traveling companions. They're worse than a strikeout-plus-one and are a sure recipe for disaster.

Yet each character hopes passively that the magical Wizard will be able to save them. They figure that somebody else can solve their problems and make them complete.

But the Scarecrow learns that to acquire knowledge and wisdom he needs to explore, then fail before succeeding, and actively mix it up with others. To find feelings, the Tin Man learns, he needs to confront and endure pain and disappointment. The Cowardly Lion, to acquire courage, learns he needs to risk, to be rebuffed and humiliated—and that what he wants most he has to give away. And in looking for security and "home," Dorothy finds out that the Wizard is a sham and a huckster and that the answers eventually lie within herself.

The path of the four companions is our path. We move closer to self-love when we become active players, take responsibility, risk, search, and quest on our own, as those that lived before us did. We need to pass that message on to others, as well as the lesson that so long as power flows only from the outside in, human life will be turned inside out.

—◦◦◦—

People with self-love recognize their limitations— not that they don't stretch; they seem to have realistic goals that put existence, expectations, and achievement in perspective. They gain by not being afraid to lose.

They take pride in doing things well, but they also recognize that sometimes "just good enough" is OK, that it's OK not to be the best, and that early failure can be turned into later success.

A friend of mine tells a story of when he was in the seventh grade. Jerry tried out for the choir. Then, as a blossoming adolescent, Jerry's voice didn't sound much better than a rusty gate on a cold night in November. The choir director, who was also the basketball coach, gently suggested, after hearing his voice, that Jerry might perhaps want to go out for the basketball team instead.

Jerry did what the choir director/coach suggested—and made the team, as the eighth man. He warmed the bench for most of the season. But he made a basket late in the year, a score he still treasures. Even though the events had taken place more than fifty years before, he told me, he remembered them today as if they had happened last week. "How gentle he was in delivering the bad news!" he said of the choir director/coach. "How he could be truthful without punishing! How it was my first experience with failure! And how it forced me to come to grips with my own limitations! And that defining event has provided an important model to me over the years."

Today Jerry is a distinguished professor of medicine. He is also a wise and kind teacher who metes out criticism with a gentleness that encourages his students to search for answers and truths. He protects their dignity. I'm sure his students feel they've been invited into the choir rather than banished from it. He passes down a legacy about the importance of self-respect every time he meets with his students.

Sometimes mothers have a sixth sense and can nip a fear in the bud and thereby promote self-esteem.

Sam told me that his parents were the most unmechanical people he'd ever met. His mother wanted to award his father the Nobel Prize for physics every time he successfully changed a lightbulb. Yet she also seemed to sense that this atmosphere, this pervasive fear of mechanics, could prove a handicap to Sam as he grew up.

When he began to show an interest in photography at age twelve, his mother bought him a 35-mm camera—an Argus C–3, he remembers still.

Sam took the camera home, and his mother told him to study the manual as if it were the Talmud. He studied everything there was to read about f-stops and shutter speeds, and by his mid-teens had mastered his "complicated machine." Sam's mother correctly assumed that his tenacity and love for learning would detoxify the family's fear of mechanics.

To this day Sam still takes good pictures. His abilities with the camera became a cornerstone in his building of self-love—recognizing that with patience, discipline, and the proper learning manuals, he did not have to be captive to his fears and limitations. From his mother, he received the legacy "Try It!" And that's what legacies are—gifts from the past that we then pass on to the future.

There are those who also have every reason not to love themselves. Many cope with those concerns every day, feeling like inconsequential bits of sand on a beach, washed away indiscriminately.

"I had many disabilities," Somerset Maugham wrote in his 1963 memoir. "I was small and had endurance but little physical strength. I had no facility for games. I stammered; I was shy . . . I had an instinctive shrinking from my fellow man that has made it difficult for me to enter into any familiarity with them . . . I have never liked anyone on first sight." There are many like Maugham who grow up feeling inferior but learn to overcome their problems and lead very successful lives.

Some events in early life can be of such toxic proportion that they can produce the very opposite of self-love: not exactly self-hatred, per se, but a pervasive fear of the world, mistrust, profound anxiety, and feelings of inadequacy, doubt, and despair.

Socrates once said that hope is a waking dream. Those with limited hope may be subject to a perpetual nightmare. Those who have been the victims of physical abuse, deception, mistrust, and fear often have no waking dreams of meadows in springtime. They second-guess themselves, and as a result, their thinking and behavior are often inconsistent and cloudy. They work hard to please others—and are tyrannized by the "shoulds" and "oughts" of their lives. They may seem outwardly assured, but they're trembling children within.

They are easily hurt. They play it safe, in part because they've conditioned themselves to expect rejection even as they constantly look for approval. Some almost court rejection—to prove to themselves in an unconscious way that they deserve all the adversity they run into. They rarely experience pleasure, because they have not learned the freedom to play, and they feel guilty enjoying themselves.

Many avoid others or surround themselves with lots of people to dilute their chances of being discovered. And still others unleash their disgust and anger at themselves in the form of self-destructive acts, body abuse, repeated accidents, excessive use of drugs, and, in the severest of situations, suicide.

"Love thy neighbor as thyself" takes on a very different meaning when you have no self-love: treating others as you treat yourself means you will treat others badly. No amount of window dressing— money, title, a degree from a good school, or an important family name—can disguise the misery of those with no hope, with no waking dreams.

But just because one has an aversion to self-love does not mean self-love cannot be sought—and found. Even the most troubled soul can be helped to recognize hope in some elusive way.

⸺ ❦ ⸺

Emily is a remarkable woman in her late twenties. She works hard at being pleasant, but beneath her thin smile she covers up a great deal of pain.

She'll tell you in the breeziest and warmest of tones how she had a privileged childhood in the traditional sense: influential parents who in their own way loved her, a wonderful home in a prestigious community, great schools, and all of the trappings associated with affluence.

But her shining veneer covers painful scars. As a child, Emily was sexually abused by her father on an almost daily basis for a number of years. Her father didn't so much threaten her with secrecy as bludgeon it into her, saying that if she ever told anyone, he would deny it and people would say she was crazy. Further compounding the situation was the fact that her mother knew what was happening all the while. "It influenced every moment of my life," Emily said, "How the kids looked at me at school; my inability to concentrate on studying; being hypersensitive to everything and not being able to laugh at jokes. I never had a safe place to be. And I always harbored the thought that maybe I was responsible."

A number of years later, living away from home, she finally confronted her mother on her silent complicity. Her mother simply urged Emily to move on and forget the past.

At that point, Emily's level of self-love was in free fall. She minimized every success and maximized every failure in her life. "I probably could give myself away for nothing and still have no takers," she said once. How one justifies such a traitorous act is nearly impossible—and she found few justifications. The whole experience, like many inhuman acts, was absurd.

Emily had a lot of reasons not to love herself. The critical building blocks of self-love—trust, fairness, respect, and intimacy—had been severely impaired and replaced by betrayal, deceit, fear, trauma, and opaque minds. Her life was consumed with rage, guilt, shame, and revenge.

Yet, remarkably, Emily refused to capitulate. Tenaciously, she held on to a solid core of spiritual values that had a powerful influence on her ability to fight the pain and give meaning to her life. She pursued artistic interests and created a beautiful environment that she could control, ever searching for healing and hope in a world that had been hostile and abusive to her.

Over time she has liberated herself from the thought that she was responsible for what happened. She works hard to let go of the pain of the past. She tries to forgive, knowing the healing must come from within—and that to hold on to the rage, however justified, will allow the perpetrator to win, will make her concentrate on herself as a victim, and will prevent her from getting on with her life. She seemed to take the words of Jean-Paul Sartre to heart: "If you want your characters to live, you must liberate them."

Self-love can be robbed from us by events we can't always control. Getting it back again is not only possible, as Emily showed, but it happens a lot of the time. And it's important to include in any legacy that there are paradoxical events where the "good lessons learned" in youth actually have a damaging impact later on.

———❦———

Natalie came to see me and described the roots of her feelings of inadequacy.

She was sent away to a highly disciplined boarding school at the age of eight. Each Friday the girls' conduct for the past week was reviewed in front of the entire faculty and student body. Everyone's name was called, and all the girls' peccadilloes for the week were read out loud and their behavior was graded as "very good," "good," or "good enough."

The mark of "very good" was given for perfect behavior, with allowance for two little "slips." The mark of "good" was given if there had been three lapses in conduct, such as being late for class, talking in class, being out of uniform, or not doing the homework. The third mark of "good enough" went to those who had talked back or been rude. "There was a fourth mark," Natalie said. "If you got that fourth mark, you were not worthy of any comment."

For nine months out of every year over nine years Natalie and her peers stood in a semicircle and had judgment passed on them. Three hundred and twenty five conduct reports. The system created was a classic lose-lose situation, where no matter how much you achieved, you would never be allowed to feel good about yourself. In this system, perfect behavior was deemed just "very good," very good behavior was demoted to "good," and anything more than three lapses in weekly conduct could become grounds for censure.

To Natalie's way of thinking after she left school, to be approved of—and accepted—meant she had to be nothing less than perfect. The scorecard the school drew for her made the possibility of her achieving self-love a practical impossibility.

Yet Natalie worked at it, and came to see that the paradigm was all wrong to start with and that "good enough" was, in fact, good enough. She came to understand that four mistakes committed in one week at age thirty did not damn her to hell.

Some, like Natalie, just get handed the wrong map in their journey to self-love. Some deal with parents who felt a compulsive need to rewrite the happy endings of Golden Books. But many find themselves able to throw away the old maps and let their own inner compasses guide them on their voyages.

We need to tell our children that to be human, we need to take chances and make mistakes. Only via this route will we develop the confidence to courageously commit ourselves.

―⟨∙⟩―

Where does self-love come from? How is it that one child nurtured by two loving parents can grow up insecure, while another child raised in a disturbed environment grows up confident and loving herself?

How does this happen? A. L. Luria, the brilliant Russian neurologist, was correct in saying, "It is vanity to dream of having a completely predictive psychology . . . Perhaps it is the best we can do as we do now: to understand what we can and have inspired ideas that lead us to observe the rest with care."

But there is no Rosetta Stone that deciphers life.

Some theories seem to bear up over time. I believe Erik Erikson was correct in saying that an early sense of trust was vital in developing self-love. He defined trust as "consistency, continuity, and sameness of experience providing a rudimentary sense of identity." But that's only a piece of the self-esteem puzzle.

We have to think of ourselves as bio-psycho-social beings. And for a significant number, we are also spiritual. We are a complex and evolving system adapting to all sorts of signals. We are multihyphenated people performing different tasks under differing circumstances—parent, child, worker, friend—and all at the same time.

We are bio-body in the sense that we all have component genes, chemicals, hormones, enzymes, and trace metals acting in concert with cells, organs, vessels, and nerves, which affect how we feel, think and act.

We are psycho-self—with a mind that outperforms the largest Cray computer as it stores, integrates, decodes and discharges trillions of bits of information involved in making instantaneous decisions. We are giant optiscans, incorporating everything that happens to us, and we give it a meaning in context.

We are social and relate to the world outside us: to parents, relatives, friends, teachers, and adversaries.

And many of us are spiritual, influenced by a belief system in which moral and ethical imperatives serve as guiding stars in directing our lives toward the destinations we want to reach, responsive to a power that transcends traditional logic.

Self-love involves the entire bio-psycho-social-spiritual spectrum and doesn't come from just one determinate. It springs from all and more. But sometimes just the little things make the difference.

Paul is a very quick-thinking, creative person who runs before he walks and finds solutions before he focuses on problems. He has a "fire-aim-ready" approach to life and possesses self-love in boundless quantities. If he's not racing, he feels he's standing still. He's one of the people for whom "no" means the negotiations are just beginning. And if he's not standing on the edge, he feels he's taking up too much space.

We met for lunch one day, and as usual he flowed over with ideas, full of optimism and chock full of notions for can't-miss deals. Yet as he spoke I noted his eyes and voice began to drift off. His thoughts and words moved inward, and his speech became barely audible. It was as if he were on two thinking tracks: one in the restaurant; the other in the ozone layer. I pointed this out to him, and he responded by telling me a story.

A very special uncle had recently died. Paul had been called upon to deliver the eulogy and was searching for ways to capture the essence of his uncle's life without sounding trite. The words came out ever so slowly. In a half-conscious, almost free-associative way, he asked, "How long does a hug last? A day? A week? A month? Forever?"

He told me of his uncle hugging him as a child— and of how he felt the warmth of his uncle's soft chest and smelled his uncle's special smell. It all seemed to convey, in that hug, a sense of trust, caring, love, warmth, specialness, and security. Not a word passed between them, and yet every time they met, they hugged with the same effect. Paul's uncle had gone, but the hug remained, and with it a memory of love that Paul carried with him as a critical buttress to his own sense of self-love.

Self-love opens us to lasting relationships. It allows us to trust and care and share. And because self-love opens us in those ways, our lives benefit enormously. We need to tell our children that, even as we try to give them all the love we're able to muster.

Unfortunately, you can't just give someone self-love. It's a lifetime job we all deal with. But you can, like Paul's uncle, create an atmosphere in which it can grow.

Thoughtful listening, allowing others to take risks, constructive criticism, genuine respect, being there in a nonjudgmental way at a time of anxiety or crisis, play a big part in allowing people to work through their difficulties and learn to trust themselves.

We are all to some degree a Joshua, comparing ourselves to others, questioning our worth, wondering if we really matter. Even Shakespeare wrote in one of his sonnets:

. . . I . . . look upon myself, and curse my fate,
Wishing me like to one more rich in hope,
Featured like him, like him with friends posses'd,
Desiring this man's art and that man's scope,
With what I most enjoy, contented least . . .

We're the only ones like us who will ever live. That's worth passing on to a son or daughter or friend. Or as Heschel wrote in 1965: "I am an average man, but to my heart I am not an average man. To my heart I am a great moment. The challenge I face is how to actualize, how to concretize the great eminence of my being."

3

LEARNING

I must study politics and war that my sons
may have liberty to study mathematics and
philosophy. My sons ought to study mathematics
and philosophy, geography, natural history,
naval architecture, navigation, commerce and
agriculture, in order to give their children
a right to study painting, poetry, music,
architecture, statuary, tapestry, and porcelain.

—*Letter from John Adams to*
Abigail Adams, May 12, 1781

The Wisdom of
the Vine

Lush vineyards and high-tech companies may seem planets apart, but in the mind of a talented leader, they are a powerful combination.

Doug runs a medium-size technology company in Silicon Valley. Two years ago he gathered his people together and gave them some disappointing news. Earnings were down, sales were flat, and the competition was breathing down their necks.

Then Doug switched to the metaphorical. He told the group a story from his home life, where he is the owner of a once-broken-down vineyard he'd bought four years before and turned from a veritable disaster into an exciting and profitable operation.

Driving home one day, he saw dark smoke about ten miles from his property. He was concerned but privately thought, "Thank God, it's not my land."

But then he saw thousands of starlings swarming out of the burning woods toward his vineyard. There were so many birds that they formed a huge black cloud—all moving in the direction of his ripening grapes.

He tried to scare them off by firing a shotgun, which he'd pulled out of the trunk of his car. But to no avail. Recognizing the battle was lost, Doug felt helpless and began to cry as he watched the starlings descend on his fields and eat his grapes.

He told his employees he'd learned a lot from that experience. He'd discovered the limits of his control. No matter how well he planned, he said, he still couldn't prevent catastrophe. Nature exercised her wisdom to determine when the grapes were ready, and the birds, in fighting for their own survival, left their danger zone and unfortunately chose a safe haven in his vineyard.

He also learned something about acceptance, Doug said. He couldn't bring back the grapes. It was simply a case of sunk cost, and there was nothing he could do about them. He just had to live with the situation and begin working toward the next season.

The group stood before him mesmerized. After he finished this story, Doug looked at them and asked them to rededicate themselves and tend to their vines. That was all they could do.

The employees left the room, elated in a strange way. They had learned that being knocked down was not the same as being knocked out. They understood that planning, hard work, and risk were essential to learning—but that even well-planned strategies are subject to events not under their limited control. They could identify with Václav Havel when he said, "The only lost cause is the one you give up, before the struggle."

—⟨᠀⟩—

Learning is necessary for our survival. It forces us to perceive anew, to light up, to grow and change and adapt. For a mind stretched to a new position, as Oliver Wendell Holmes said, never returns to the same place. Stretching the mind is an antidote to staleness and boredom.

Learning helps us cope with unpredictability. It is a process the Romans understood exactly—that to educate is to *ex-ducare*, to "lead out," to open new channels. Learning teaches us that the formulaic response—the right/wrong pat answer—is not necessarily the right one and that the ultimate goal of learning is to adapt, connect, and build up a storehouse we might need to raid in a famine year. Call it wisdom. Some do. I call it the ability to separate truth from facts.

Wisdom based on learning takes many forms. I have a friend with a distinguished career who recently told a group at the Boston Latin School that the best thing he'd learned at the oldest public school in the United States was that to have a messy paper was to have a messy mind. He'd applied that wisdom in every successful business deal he'd made in forty years, and it has worked.

I know a man who keeps a gold star on his refrigerator. He earned it at the age of fifty-five when he decided it was time he learned to type; the was star awarded to him by his teacher after the completion of the course. To him it was proof that we never stop learning, and that we carry the ability to learn throughout our days. He shows it to his grandchildren proudly. A legacy.

Socrates felt that the strength of his wisdom was his awareness of how little he knew. He had mastered the philosophy of "learned ignorance." That's why I admire people who are troubled at times by ambiguities, who thoughtfully struggle with complex problems and resist the urge to give knee-jerk responses to hard, unanswerable questions, of which there are many in life, and who possess a sense of wonder and awe in their lives.

We all learn and work differently, and it is important to figure out what works best for us. Robert Frost wrote best at night, Balzac wrote in a monk's habit, and Shiller wrote with rotten apples on his desk. Thomas Wolfe tapped out *Look Homeward Angel* on a typewriter perched atop his refrigerator, the six-foot eight-inch writer standing the entire time. As the fox said in Antoine de Saint-Exupéry's *The Little Prince*, "It is only with the heart that one can see rightly; what is essential is invisible to the eye." That's the kind of learning that relies on instinctive understanding honed by years of experience.

A true learner is an explorer and a discoverer, using his tools to mine bits of treasure. And when he doesn't hit pay dirt, he presses on, heeding the words of Wallace Stevens, and "After the final No there comes a Yes and on that Yes, the future of the world depends."

When I was a pre-med undergraduate, grades were very important. Medical schools required a better than decent grade in organic chemistry, physics, and other sciences as part of the price of admission. I spent an inordinate amount of time studying calculus and memorizing formulas. At the end of my junior year, I came home from college and was greeted by a big smile from my mother. I'd aced the calculus exam—yet I felt curiously hollow.

In truth, I was grade smart, not course smart. I had an excellent memory and an ability to look at a problem, dredge out the right formula, plug in the appropriate numbers, and get the right answer. Getting the right answer and a good grade was my goal. Not learning. In the words of the old song, "It don't mean a thing if you ain't got the swing." Just the answer without the meaning is one pulseless song.

I was learning without understanding or integration, as if I were stocking grain in silos somewhere in Nebraska. It's the kind of learning called "banked learning."

The active teacher deposits the data (currency) in the head (bank) of the passive learner. The material remains there, static, like a noninterest-bearing note. At exam time, the teacher asks a question, the student withdraws the deposit, and if there is a match between the deposit and the withdrawal, the student receives a high grade. But few people ask the important question: has the student really "learned" anything?

Clearly, certain kinds of banked learning are important. We need to know multiplication tables, distances between cities, birthdays, and foreign currency exchange rates just as practical matters in order to get by in the modern world. But banked learning for its own sake is like learning in a cul-de-sac—it doesn't lead anywhere.

Real learning, which has a three-dimensional working value, is known as "connected learning." It's the kind of learning that fosters and encourages judgment through seeing patterns and relationships. It's like putting high-test gas in a quality car and feeling the surge as you drive uphill.

Connected learners recognize that most problems are not either/or propositions. They weigh relative merits and probabilities and don't recite formulas. They connect one set of values and properties with another and decide which is better or more reasonable. Connected learners reconcile seeming contradictions and attempt to make sense of them.

The sport of rowing is a good metaphor for understanding how learning works.

The oarsmen's actions divide into four parts, the "catch," the "drive," "the finish," and the "recovery."

First comes the catch. Eight oarsmen swing their arms and shoulders wide—four to starboard and four to port—and slash their oar blades into the water to "catch" the water.

Then follows the drive, during which the eight oarsmen push back with their legs, hitch their shoulders, and pull as hard as they can on their oars.

Then there's the finish, at the end of the stroke. The oarsmen lean back in their seats with their oar handles in their laps, pause, feather the oar blades, and then "recover" in preparation for the next stroke.

The beauty of this exercise to all the oarsmen is

the knowledge that the boat actually does most of its traveling when there are no oars in the water—when nobody's doing anything but preparing for the next moment. The period of doing nothing is as crucial as the period of doing something. Reflection is a necessary prelude to effective action, or, as Wallace Stevens wrote, "Perhaps the truth depends upon a walk around the lake."

That's learning. We travel farther when we pause—to incubate, think, reflect, distill, digest, and connect. We need to help people understand that a pause in the road doesn't mean the end of a journey.

⸻

Learners are curious. They ask "Why?" Good learners have an ability to recognize patterns and see metaphors where others see merely trees or sand on the beach. And that's why it's important to see the difference between data, information, knowledge and wisdom. As Nobel Prize recipient Albert Szent-Györgyi put it: "Research is to see what everyone else has seen, and to think what nobody else has thought." Seeing is believing, but believing is also seeing.

Data, for example, is undigested information and observations: the average daily rainfall in London; the number of chickens produced in Arkansas in 1966. Data is isolated, static, and old. Or, as one friend of mine insightfully calls raw facts, "a partially evolving view, from a partially evolving somewhere, by a partially evolving somebody."

Information is organized data. It permits us to

classify things into common groups: two-legged animals, chemicals with the same valence, cars with similar horsepower. Packaging things into categories gives us the advantage of using data in effective ways. It is the beginning of connective learning.

Knowledge is organized information. It's based on intense study and experience, and calls up and correlates the data and information that we have built up over time. The knowledgeable person has at his or her disposal a range of intelligent choices that can lead him or her to decisions based on the best probabilities and combinations of information. Knowledgeable people see the big picture and understand not only the connections between data and information but the disconnection as well.

Wisdom is an elusive phenomenon. It's a kind of cognitive alchemy—a mixture of disparate data, information, and knowledge escaping black holes. It is the ability not only to know right from wrong but also to apply common sense solutions to issues even when you don't have all the knowledge. Wisdom transcends disciplinary barriers. It may be separate from formal education or even experience—the sort of just plain common sense that automatically adds twenty points to an IQ. Like water vapor, wisdom is hard to get hold of, but when it's there, you know it.

As one of the great physicians of the twentieth century, Sir William Osler, wrote: "To study the phenomena of disease without books is to sail an uncharted sea, while to study books without patients is not to go to sea at all." Wisdom, to be effective, needs study and application, theory, and practice.

We cannot be taught wisdom; we have to discover it for ourselves through journeys that no one can undertake for us, and often at great peril. "Bravo!" Rhett Butler said to Scarlett O'Hara in *Gone With the Wind*. "Now you are beginning to think for yourself instead of letting others think for you. That's the beginning of wisdom."

Charlie, as his friends called him, arrived at my office one morning and asked if he should give up smoking.

Before me stood a bony, thin, small man in his mid-seventies who was having difficulty breathing and who coughed spasmodically. He'd had a distinguished career as a professor of economics and had pioneered a major area of study in his field. At the time, though, he had retired, lost his wife, and was playing host to three primary cancers—prostate, blood, and lung.

He was lonely but managed to make the most of each day and was in the process of putting the final touches on a career autobiography. He told me that he went through three to four packs of unfiltered Lucky Strikes a day. I asked, "Do you like smoking?"

"I love it," he said.

"How long have you smoked?"

"Since I was fifteen."

"Then why give it up?" I replied.

A knowing smile crossed his face, and he said, "I knew you'd have some common sense. That's why I came to see you. I went to another doctor yesterday and he told me to stop." Clearly he had come to the right place to hear the answer he wanted to hear.

Was I wise? I like to think so. When scientific knowledge collides with real life, then everything you know carries less weight than the simple sensitivity to the needs of one lonely life. That's the conundrum (with only approximate solutions) we have to pass down to our children for them to contemplate so they can understand the difficulty of seeking and finding wisdom.

We also need to tell those who follow that there are limits to what you can learn—that no matter how much we learn, it is still incomplete and approximate.

The New York Times reported almost thirty years ago that if the average reader tried to keep up with one year's output from learned scientific publications, it would take that person fifty years of reading, twenty-four hours a day, seven days a week. And that was in 1970. Imagine how long it would take to read today's output.

An esteemed boss of mine once told me that it would require a minimum of ten years of reading, study, and clinical experience to become an expert in our field. Being young and impatient, I assumed I could do it faster. Ten years later I appreciated his message. He had underestimated the time. It would take me a lifetime.

Good learners spend a lifetime stretching and

dealing with their frustrations as they learn. A friend who took up golf in his mid-seventies spent most of the dewy early mornings slicing round white balls into the woods. For him it became a challenge to learn how to get the little white ball into the white cup on the big green. He learned as much about himself as he did about the mechanics of a golf swing. His intolerance for failure—combined with his need to set realistic expectations—meant he kept learning.

A colleague of mine gave up a tenured professorship to pursue a career in opera because he didn't want to retire from academia feeling he "blew it" by not pursuing what his soul cried out to do.

Other colleagues have gone back to school on the sly to dip into courses that were too threatening and difficult when they were younger. Kierkergaard. Joyce. Milton. They all did so with the purpose of taking on a new challenge, with the hope that maybe they'd find a hidden talent or that they'd simply broaden themselves beyond their present scopes. They didn't take academic courses. They were taking life experiences.

Together, they seemed to understand that the mind, like a muscle, needs exercise to stay fit. And that's something we need to pass on to our children.

—◦◦—

There are as many different muscles in our bodies as there are smarts in our minds.

There are mechanical smarts and spatial relationship smarts. There are people with extraordinary interpersonal smarts and people who can play music and pick up languages without much effort. And there are aesthetic smarts, street smarts, and ownership smarts—the special ability to know a field so thoroughly as to be able to decode its mystery and "own" it in all its dimensions. But nobody corners the market on smarts.

Kenneth Olson founded Digital Equipment Company in the 1940s and built it into one of the most successful manufacturers of supercomputers in the world. The proudest watchword at the company was that no one, not a single soul, had ever been laid off. DEC was a model firm.

Yet in 1977 Olson went before a gathering of "futurists" and told the assembly that "there is no reason for any individual to have a computer in his home." By 1982 one million homes had computers. DEC became a limited player in the computer wars. The company was later sold to Compaq and shortly thereafter came the announcement that fifteen thousand DEC employees would be laid off.

On July 10, 1977, Consolidated Edison Chairman Charles Luce went before an assembly of business leaders in Manhattan and told them, "The Con Edison system is in the best shape in fifteen years, and there's no problem about the summer." Three days later the system crashed and a twenty-four-hour blackout threw New York City into chaos.

Bad judgment? No smarts? Not necessarily. Given the data and information Olson and Luce had available to them at the time, they were probably right. There are just no such things as guarantees. Smarts change, and one has to remain hypervigilant to keep up with the trends. And Olson and Luce also serve as a reminder that the best of us, if we stay in the game long enough—and stretch—we'll all wind up with egg on our faces.

⟋⟋⟍⟋

One night about ten years ago I went to see the Celtics play at the old Boston Garden. After Larry Bird made a sensational shot, I jumped out of my seat and shouted to a friend, "Bird's fantastic! He's a genius!" My friend, a bright academic, replied, "Yeah he's great, but I heard he's not that smart."

I was floored by his comment. After I regained my composure, I said, "You've got to be kidding. If I were starting a team, I certainly wouldn't pick Albert Einstein as my power forward! I'd pick Larry Bird. No one but him!" But Bird was only a dumb jock to my friend, even though we'd just seen him define new laws of physics, and kinesiology in one long run up the court that took all of ten seconds.

All smarts are relative and don't automatically transfer to other areas. Good writers are not necessarily good speakers—and summa grads are not expected to hit three-point jumpers from twenty-five feet.

We also need to learn not to let our natural prejudices take over and influence our decision making.

I received a letter from a dentist colleague about a little old Jewish man with a thick European accent, dressed in a rumpled suit, who came to the hospital to have his teeth cleaned. He had been referred to the dental clinic by his son, a member of the hospital staff.

The dentist spent the entire appointment talking about what a wonderful doctor the old man's son was.

After a while, with not a small degree of irritation, the old man said, "I'm not so bad myself, you know." Recognizing that he had slighted the man, the dentist said, "I'm sure you've done some special things. Tell me about them." The tone of his voice must have been disingenuous, more of an obligatory request than real curiosity on the dentist's part.

The old man proceeded to tell the dentist, in a very slow way, how he had been born in the Ukraine . . . emigrated to the United States in the early 1900s . . . became a scientist. . . . He was drawing the whole thing out, torturing the dentist. "Then I discovered something called . . . streptomycin . . . for which I won the Nobel Prize in 1941."

Dr. Selman Waksman had made his presence known.

We can tell our children not to mess with little old Jewish men, as my dentist friend recounted in mortification in his letter. Or we can tell them that learning doesn't always wear a power suit, smell of Old Spice, and have a British accent. Or we can tell them that talent has no gender, color, age, or appearance and that stereotyping is a form of antilearning that prevents us from developing meaningful relationships and limits our ability to grow. It creates the illusion of know-ing—and merely reinforces ignorance, which is not so much a lack of knowledge as it is operating on false knowledge.

———❧❧———

Linus Pauling, the winner of two Nobel Prizes, was once asked how he could do so much with what he knows. "I'm not sure," he replied. "I just seem to get rid of the material in my head that doesn't make much sense." His real talent, in fact, was to have access to a vast storehouse of material and a capacity to connect, prioritize, and differentiate what was available to him. He could see different kinds of logic in the differing connections. He was the very opposite of the man with only a hammer in his toolbox, to whom everything looks like a nail.

Real learning and wisdom, I often think, is the ability to think nimbly and metaphorically. That means crossing disciplines and boundaries. That kind of exercise stimulates a sense of imagination and won-der, which helps us come up with novel possibilities and solutions.

"Inflation," Theodore H. White wrote, "is the dis-ease of money, the cancer of modern civilization, and the leukemia of planning and hope. "One sentence that borrows images from economics, history, medicine, and religion helps us understand the problem all the better because of the imagery. Teaching our children to think—and learn—across disciplines would be a wonderful gift. Real learners own the subject—and can treat it as malleable clay, ready to shape it into any form or image they want. It wasn't a coincidence that Teddy White, a master learner, was also a master imagist.

Conversely, we often find wisdom in unlikely places and by accident.

My wife, an interior designer, and I often spend fall weekends traveling to antique fairs around New England, wandering through the stalls and admiring the wares under slanted September sunlight that is unique for its brightness.

One Saturday afternoon I was among the old cribbage boards (I collect them) when my wife marched up to find me. A dealer was selling two Queen Anne chairs, she said, perfect for her most recent client, but the dealer was asking five hundred dollars apiece for them. She'd tried to negotiate with him, but he refused. Could I, she asked, negotiate with him?

This was a classic lose-lose situation if ever there was one, I said. If I didn't get the chairs, I'd feel lousy because I still wanted to be her hero. If I did get the chairs, my wife might feel bad: I'd be showing up her negotiating techniques as inferior to mine. She agreed with my logic, and we both laughed. "You're right," she said. "But try anyway."

Sucker that I am, I agreed and went over to the dealer. Would he be willing to negotiate the five hundred dollars price tag? I asked.

Absolutely not, he said.

I launched into a short monologue about how everything is negotiable, but his face remained as cold as the New Hampshire granite around us.

"Fella," he said, "These chairs are not negotiable. Five hundred dollars. They were five hundred for her," gesturing toward my wife, "and they're five hundred for you." But then a thought hit me. "Would you take six hundred for them?"

"I only want five hundred."

"But would you take six hundred?" I asked.

"Of course."

"Then they are negotiable," I said.

"Eh-yuh," he agreed, puzzled.

"So you're telling me they're negotiable up but not down." He agreed with my logic but not with my price, and he looked at me strangely.

I'd like to say that I got him to lower his price and that I walked away doubly a hero—winner of the chairs and winner of a contest in logic. But five hundred dollars was his rock-solid price. I didn't get the chairs, but I did not feel defeated. Quite the contrary. When I realized that negotiations could move in both directions, I learned that losing and winning can happen at the same time—you can win an intellectual argument and lose a negotiation all in the same breath.

We all have our own sense of logic, which influences our learning and the way we think. What makes sense to one person may make no sense to another.

For example, I was once at a party and a man came up to me and asked me what I thought of zinc. I figured he was a commodities trader, but it turned out he wanted to talk about the value of taking zinc supplements and their impact on longevity.

Now zinc occurs naturally in the body, and he

believed that people who take additional zinc live longer. His logic, though fuzzy to my mind—since longevity is determined by far more than one-shot metal infusions—was simple and iron-clad in his mind. I knew there would be no point in even contesting his view. He had "learned" the truth.

Sometimes we distort what we perceive, and learn what we distort, and in the process fool ourselves. It's important to understand how we know what we know, and to have the flexibility to "unlearn."

There's much we need to learn and pass on.

We need to learn what motivates us. We need to learn to link with others and take advantage of their special wisdom and smarts. True learners learn more about themselves when they learn more about others.

We need to learn to understand life-cycle events, like birth, marriage, raising kids, and success and failure. And we need to learn to revere life in all its forms. I used to think nothing of tearing a leaf off a bush until a friend admonished me, asking how I'd feel if someone came along and yanked a chunk of hair out of my head. It stopped my hostile assault on nature immediately.

We need to learn more about other cultures and languages as the world becomes increasingly connected and condensed, and we need to learn more about demographic trends and to anticipate how they are going to influence our future.

We need to learn to defend against an attitude that

"seals the mind against imagination and the heart against experience," as Edith Wharton put it in *The Age of Innocence*. We need, in other words, to learn to hold on to the awe of the child and the courage of the warrior—to risk, have fun, fail, and come back again for more. To find the work we're good at and that excites us.

And as we continue to make greater use of technology in our daily lives, we need to learn that the human mind still quarterbacks the operation, that it exercises the judgment, and that it ultimately bears the responsibility for decisions and actions.

"We cannot know the consequences of our own best actions," Stuart Kaufman wrote recently. "All we players can do is be locally wise, not globally wise. All we can do is hitch up our pants, put on our galoshes, and get on with it the best we can. Only God has the wisdom to understand the final law, the throws of the quantum dice." We need to learn perspective: that we can clean up the world tomorrow, but just settle for cleaning our rooms today; that a mistake is an event for which a solution has not yet been found; and that, as George Will put it, there is a beginning, a *muddle*, and an end to all projects.

And most important, we need to learn a sense of humility—and to not think of ourselves as such hotshots. As Peter Drucker has pointed out, the so-called information revolution we're in the midst of today is actually the fourth such revolution in the history of mankind. The first was the invention of writing some five thousand years ago in Mesopotamia. The second was the invention of the written book thirteen hundred years ago. The third was the invention of movable type by Johannes Gutenberg five hundred years ago. Yes, we are as smart as we think we are. But no, we're merely taking advantage of gifts we've received from the past, improving on them, and giving them to those who follow us. As the Romans said, *"Nova Ex Veteris"*—"The new must be born out of the old."

If we pass on to our children a sense that all our wisdom has brought us to the conclusion that we're not so wise after all, that is wisdom enough.

There is much to learn from one another, for it's what we learn, after we know it all, that really counts.

4

LABORING

In the end, more than they wanted freedom, they wanted security. They wanted a comfortable life, and they lost it all, security, comfort, and freedom. When the Athenians finally wanted not to give to society, but for society to give to them, when the freedom they wished for most was freedom from responsibility, the Athenians ceased to be free.

—*Edith Hamilton*

The 4-T Work Diet

The Toyota factory in Nagoya, Japan, is as large as a small city. Walking though it one day, I noted identical banners that seemed everywhere. I asked my guide what the words meant.

He said to look at the people. I saw a symphony of mechanics, each with a role, tied into those behind and in front of them. He told me how the workers were expected to use their judgment in planning their work schedules and that they kept diaries to note problems on the line. They had to discuss their findings and recommendations at preplanned meetings.

I appreciated his comments, but I pointed up again at the cloth flags hanging from the rafters. "But, what do the banners say?" I asked.

"The Mind is Power," he said, and I understood instantly. Toyota wanted to reinforce the importance of dignity, collaboration, and empowerment, all leading toward pride in the work environment. It meant Toyota understood that those who work with their hands are just as important as those who work with their minds, and that judgment and decision-making pay off on the factory floor as well as they do in the executive suite. The company was being cost-effective as well as care-effective. They understood that it's the man that honors the work and not the work that honors the man.

―――― ⌒⌒ ――――

"Everyone's work," wrote Samuel Butler in *The Way of All Flesh*, "whether it be literature or music or pictures or architecture, is always a portrait of himself or herself."

The average person spends at least forty years of his or her life at work. That's about ten thousand days and around eighty thousand hours, not counting commuting, overtime, worrying, and weekends. Not surprisingly, work is the most important activity that defines people's lives. Yet work is a two-sided coin.

For many, work represents the single most important source of self-affirmation, constructive engagement, accomplishment, and intellectual satisfaction. Work allows us to channel and sublimate our competitive, aggressive needs. We "tackle" a problem, "grapple" with new material, "make a killing" in the market, or "knock the competition dead"—without having to put on football pads or buy Ninja sticks.

Not surprisingly, work also is a constant source of vexation, pain, anguish, and heartburn for many people. It's no accident that repeated surveys show that what people want most at work is to be treated with dignity and respect, to be rewarded appropriately, to be housed in a safe environment, to be given a chance to grow and stretch, and to share their ideas with other talented colleagues. People seem to understand, too, that a first-rate mind likes to work with another first-rate mind. And that a second-rate mind will seek out a third-rate mind.

Two "diets" represent as clearly as possible what we find most repugnant about work—and they're not all that uncommon.

Recently I visited a busy advertising office. The place appeared to be in total chaos. People were running in all directions, screaming at one another but not listening. Half the people in the office appeared to be high on speed, while the other half looked like they were working up to it.

A middle-aged woman caught me. Her speech was hurried and loud. Her movements were short and jerky.

"Too much work, too little time," she said. "Too many constituencies, not enough help. Too many 'to do' orders, not enough directions. Too much responsibility, not enough accountability. Too much criticism, not enough rewards. Nobody cares. No focus, no prioritization, no help, no light at the end of the tunnel. And no leadership." I expected this woman to start hyperventilating in front of me.

"But I've learned to cope with all of this," she said, after taking a deep breath. "I've been on the 4-T work diet for the past two years. And I manage to hang in there."

"What on earth is a 4-T work diet," I asked.

"Oh, it's simple." She smiled. "Tums, Tylenol, Tagamet, and Thorazine. Tums for the constant rumbling in my stomach. Tylenol for my headaches.

Tagamet for the ulcers I've developed over the past several years. And Thorazine for my nerves." Clearly a fifth T was imminent—the Time bomb ticking away and about to implode.

Is that a legacy we want to leave?

An acquaintance who ran a chain of weekly newspapers told me how, after three years at the job, he started receiving compliments from the staff on how his physique had changed. He'd lost weight—perhaps twenty pounds, he said. He'd stopped drinking beer, but that was only part of the reason behind the weight loss. The rest he attributed to the "Suburban Newspaper Editor Stress Diet," which he described as a complete loss of appetite for anything except caffeine while fending off assaults from his publisher, advertising reps, advertisers, disgruntled readers, and the complaints of grossly underpaid reporters, and the ownership, which wanted to pay the reporters even less.

He quit, realizing that a diet of battery acid and bile wasn't going to lengthen his life but rather would shorten it.

We need to pass on the fact that sometimes we have to say: "Nothing you could ever pay me is worth this amount of aggravation"—and then have the courage to leave.

―⁓⁓―

Work brings out our better side—creativity, imagination, nurturing, and mentoring. But it also forces us to deal with the darker side of our nature on a daily basis—feelings of jealousy, embarrassment, failure, envy, anger, despair, resentment, and revenge.

Maybe that's why I sometimes laugh inwardly when somebody tells me his or her company is "just like one big family." "Which kind?" I find myself asking, "The happy nuclear one or the dysfunctional bickering kind?"

Work once seemed a source of security and predictability if one used a microscope rather than a telescope to understand its dynamics. Granted, in the past a young man could graduate from high school, go to work at a local company, and reasonably expect to remain there for the next forty years and retire with a predictable pension. But those who see the "good old days" only through rose-colored glasses engage in a kind of retrospective falsification. They act as if there never was a *Tobacco Road* depicting the helpless migrant workers, or an Upton Sinclair's *Jungle* focusing on the toll on meat packers, or a *Gentlemen's Agreement* and its theme of prejudice, or an *Organization Man* and the tradeoff of security for conformity.

At one point we could pass on the mantra "work hard, stay loyal, keep your nose to the grindstone, and you'll be safe and secure." That is no longer the case. Gone are the days when the Dustin Hoffman character in the 1968 film *The Graduate* could hear one word—*plastics*—and follow the sure road to professional success. All companies experience a lifecycle—some thrive and give birth to other companies, others downsize, merge, limp along, or disappear.

Information technology has had a profound effect on the way we work. Breakthroughs in new fields like quantum electronics, information theory, and biogenetic engineering, to mention only a few, have created entire new industries in less than a generation. Meanwhile, lawyers find themselves commodities, doctors compete with HMOs, and architects have been replaced by computer-aided design. Banks compete with mutual funds for deposits. The Big Eight accounting firms are now the Big Five. Hospitals are closing inpatient units and merging so rapidly that at one point in Boston in the mid-nineties, the health care community resembled a flock of pelicans in a mating dance, so eager were the different hospitals to find a merger partner.

New terms have joined the lexicon. Now we talk of golden handcuffs and parachutes, of white knights, poison pills, and workers with blue, white, pink, and tight collars. It would take a separate book to list the new terms spawned by the computer age.

Today, innovation has become the most important factor in determining whether a person has security on the job—because only companies that innovate will survive in an globally competitive marketplace. Today the mantra is "innovate or emigrate"—and that's become true for individual jobs as well as whole companies.

And partly as a result of this change in the traditional worldview, the old command and control management structure has gone the way of *Tyrannosaurus Rex*. If imagination, intellectual capital, and innovation count for more in today's working world, then it stands to reason that durability, seniority, and adherence to tradition will count for less. So the old structures have largely been replaced by less hierarchical matrix systems where people at all levels act interdependently. To many, this departure seems chaotic and confusing. They feel deceived and angry, trying to figure out where the system went wrong and how they can fix it. But we can't go home again, if home means the same old ways.

Nevertheless, some of work's life "truths" remain true, like those presented by my wise colleague Ralph Siu, who has managed to combine Eastern philosophy with modern management.

His guides for "Work Planning" include:

- The bird hunting the locust is unaware of the hawk hunting him. (Never be complacent.)
- In shallow waters, shrimps make fools of dragons. (Know your territory.)
- Don't try to catch two frogs with one hand. (Set priorities and be flexible.)
- Give the bird room to fly. (Empower your people.)

And his guides for "Work Operations" are:

- Do not insult the crocodile until you have crossed the river. (Timing and judgment are everything.)

- It is better to struggle with a sick jackass than carry the wood alone. (Delegate.)
- Do not throw a stone at a mouse and break the precious vase. (Focus and channel anger.)
- It is not the last blow of the ax that fells the tree. (Anticipate and deal with problems early.)
- The great executive not only brings home the bacon but also the applesauce. (You can work hard, but make time for the sweets.)

Even though it's a new work world, moving at the speed of light and crashing through traditional solar systems, some principles remain as sound as they ever were. And that's a legacy we need to pass on, a lesson we've received from our forebears and that we need to give to our children.

⟶ ⟨᠄᠄⟩ ⟵

But there is an exciting upside to this new paradigm: Work today forces people to be as alert, nimble and risk-oriented as possible, as we spawn new industries and opportunities all the time.

Visit a Sumerian text from five thousand years ago and compare it to, say, a San Francisco newspaper during the Gold Rush of 1849. Both would tell of wheeled transport, sailing ships, hand-held writing implements, brick molds, metallurgy, baked pottery, and the arch and vault form of construction. They would both tell of expanded farming communities and a search for gold.

What's different today is our level of expectation—and the speed with which we can transmit knowledge. The cork is out of the bottle, and the genie of change, experimentation, and possibility has escaped, never to be pushed back. As the playwright Tom Stoppard wrote: "It's the best possible time to be alive, when almost everything you thought you knew is wrong."

⌒⌒

We don't only work in organizations. We live there. Physically, mentally, emotionally, and spiritually. Without some kind of meaning and purpose to our work lives, we feel lost and floating through space. We don't want to be like Mark Twain's Widder, who "eats by the bell, goes to bed by the bell, gets up by the bell. Everything so awful and regular a body can't stand it."

When work is exciting and creative, people become focused, invested, energized, and productive. They add value to invigorate the people. Four work scenarios from my youth spring to mind.

There was Manuel, the cigar man. I used to sit for hours with my nose glued to his window, watching him hand-roll cigars and then add his own homemade glue—spit—to the last wrapper. Then he'd hold up every sculpted creation and marvel at its design and quality. He'd gently place it down on his work table like a piece of Belleek china.

Then there was Lily, the chicken lady, who could surgically and systematically pluck the feathers off a chicken on her lap in minutes—all with an economy of motion while sharing every opinion under the stars with her entranced customers.

And there was Lotzie, the Hungarian artist. I'd walk down the street to his small apartment, take a seat, and watch him paint, mesmerized by the cigarette glued to his lower lip. He specialized in elves, in all sorts of situations, and he hummed as he painted them, totally absorbed in their busy lives.

Finally, there was Sophie, the pickle lady. I'd go to school early several days a week in order to drop by her store. I'm convinced to this day that her right arm was pickled to the elbow, as she spent so much time reaching down into the cold brine to extract her treasures. I'd watch her hand emerge from the pickle juice when she'd found just the right one for me, her special customer.

My four role models created a unique sense of self through work. They felt valued, competent, involved and had control and pride over what they did. They engaged the customer, too, and created a feedback system that applauded them and made them feel better about their work and themselves.

We live in a time when the bar has been raised. Our ancestors would be awed at how we have tried to condense and juggle so many important roles and constituencies into one day. Work, family, marriage, self, community, all are expected to be performed at the highest level and subject to enormous guilt when we fall short.

Carolyn is a very competent woman in her mid-thirties who works in the research and development department of a high-tech company. She is part of the new breed, the classic juggler trying to do it all: a manager with an impossible work schedule, a devoted wife of an overly involved husband, an officer in a local charity, a gourmet cook, a voracious reader, and a devoted daughter.

She recently delivered her first child and sent out this birth announcement:

> The Greens announce an important new product, Stephanie Green 1 (SG–1). Introduced on the 9th of November, the SG–1 surprised the competition by being produced several days prior to its planned delivery date. The product managers for the SG–1, being new at this business, commented they had really babied this one along.
>
> The primary features of the SG–1 include the following:
>
> Two hands extremely useful for removing things from tables or clutching items such as hair or noses . . .

Another friend, a venture capitalist, greeted the birth of his first granddaughter with a similar announcement. It came in a square cream envelope, the size of a large wedding invitation. Inside was a stiff card that at first looked like the kind of "tombstone" ad you see in the back pages of the Finance section of *The Wall Street Journal*:

JKB/MKB
The announcement appears as a matter of
record only. Robin Leah
6 lbs 6 oz
Facility initiated, placed privately and
managed by Jessica Vaughn and
Matthew Leiberman.
Boston
Delighted Grandparents Janet and
Marvin Britcher
Montreal
November 5, 1996 9:31

Work and family have become so intertwined that
Carolyn and the grandfather have come to see a lot of
what they do though the prism of work. Yet the reality
remains that in our lives we need to strike a fine balance between the forces of work and family. That may
be the greatest challenge of the next century—to estab-
lish priorities, maintain control, analyze tradeoffs, and
manage precious time. William Butler Yeats said that
"meaningful work is not the filling of a pail but the
lighting of a fire." Carolyn and my friend obviously
see their work lives as lighting fires. Their enthusiasm
for their work comes through in their choice of
metaphors in describing important events in their lives.

That's an important legacy to pass on: if you're
filling pails from nine to five, the rest of your day isn't
going to seem much better. But if you're lighting fires,
the chances are that work and family have the potential to create a warm and eternal flame.

⎯⎯⎯⎯ ⌒⌒ ⎯⎯⎯⎯

The great physicist Freeman Dyson recalled his mother's advice as he was setting off on his career. "She begged me not to lose my humanity," he noted years later. "'You will regret it deeply,' she said, 'when one day you are a great scientist and wake up to find that you have never had time to make friends. What good will it do you to prove the Riemann Hypothesis if you have no wife or no children to share your triumph? You will find that even mathematics will grow stale and bitter if that is the only thing you are interested in.'"

The ancient Chinese had a proverb: A mouse with but one hole is easily taken. We need to tell our children in this connected, changing world that learning the skills to keep their options open will be the key to lighting fires and not filling pails—that employability, not employment, is the key to security.

A seasoned pro once told me to learn from the mistakes of others. And then, with a twinkle in his eye, he said "because you can't live long enough to make them all on your own." We need to pass on some common red flags about early, mid, and late work life.

We can't afford to be myopic in a changing work world. It's not a coincidence that *career* is derived from the French *carríere*—a racing course. Think of that association with the way we talk about people at work: being on the fast track, a slow starter, the rat race—all the time navigating obstacles with winners and losers.

A mistake many people make when entering the workforce is failing to identify their personal talents and market them inside and outside the organization.

Success in the workforce at a young age requires perspective. It requires the combination of *differentiation*— with an emphasis on the "I"—and *integration*— with an emphasis on the "We." That I/We balance involves a maturity born out of observation, risk, judgment, patience, and wisdom.

A young Austrian immigrant fleeing Hitler's *anschlüss* wangled himself a job as a copy boy in the foreign news department at *Time* magazine during the early 1940s. One of his jobs was to carry the writers' mimeographed stories from the duplicator at the typists' station on one side of the Time-Life Building to the foreign editor on the other side.

The young Henry Anatole Grunwald always made that trip very slowly—because he was reading, dissecting, and editing those "blues" in his head as he walked. And he arrived at the foreign editor's desk with a list of suggestions on how to make the story better. He called attention to himself—but did so in the context of benefiting the magazine. Grunwald later became editor-in-chief of all Time, Inc. publications.

Young people entering the workforce need to know that networking is paramount. But they also need to appreciate that good mentors are as rare as hens' teeth and that *political* is not a dirty word. Any organization with more than one person is political—

as is any family where kids jockey for attention. But at the end of the day talent must take precedence over politics if the company is going to thrive.

We also need to pass on to those just entering the workforce that advancement takes time. "Nothing great is created suddenly," the ancient Greeks said, "any more than a bush of grapes or a fig. Let it first blossom; then bear fruit; then ripen."

Or, as a wise Cape Town entrepreneur gruffly explained to his "mentee," who was forty-three at the time: "Boy, understand that you can't chop down every tree in Africa and that it takes a long time to walk from Cape Town to Cairo."

Some make false assumptions and decisions during mid-career that hamstring them and debilitate them in various ways.

They thumb through alumni magazines envious of the achievements of their colleagues. Untold numbers of people have been through my office who mention in more than mere passing that so-and-so is now a VP and that "I'm still just a GM."

Why buy into titles that may have been placed by a PR firm in two-dimensional sentences? Knowing a single thing about another person, however true, doesn't tell you a whole lot about the roundness of that person's life. Most likely it's our fantasies running wild. These blurbs are snapshots, not full-length features. And beside, would you really change places if you knew all the facts.

We also need to pass along the fact that one of the

great career mistakes is playing the numbers game—
assuming that anyone near forty-five is over the hill.
The disease of ageism is self-inflicted. It allows others
to dictate and define what *you* can and cannot do
rather than allowing *you* to determine what you can
do. Remember: you can't teach an old horse new
tricks—but there are certain tricks only an old horse
can do.

Many in mid-career fail to keep up with industry
changes or try to play the new game with outdated
equipment—technological or intellectual. Similarly,
they fail to take care of themselves physically or psychologically and look—and act—tired and worn out.
The smart ones figure out ways to refuel themselves.
And we need to pass that on.

Others in mid-career come to view work "hun-
kered down like a jackass in a hail storm," to quote
Lyndon Johnson. And that is a mistake. They remind
me of the Shel Silverstein poem:

I'd rather play tennis than go to the dentist.
I'd rather play soccer than go to the doctor.
I'd rather play hurk than go to work.
Hurk? Hurk? What's Hurk?
I don't know, but it must be better than work.

Not long ago I had lunch with a group of mid-
level managers at a company I work with regularly.
Out of the blue, one of them turned to me and said
that Jack, who was not in the room, was not a real

manager. He had no balls. He had no focus. He held meetings about holding meetings and spent a good deal of his time reorganizing agendas and delaying decisions. He didn't play to win. He played not to lose.

"He's so worried about being fired that he fakes his way through the day," this colleague said of Jack. "He's managing at half-mast. We see him as an Approximate Manager."

It was a strong indictment of a coworker, and unfortunately, they were correct. Jack was going through life in the mode of "dynamic conservatism." He had his right foot firmly on the accelerator and his left foot firmly on the brake—so that he generated a lot of noise and smoke but absolutely no movement. He merely tried to give the appearance of doing something.

And the interesting thing is, such an idea is not new.

"We trained hard, but it seemed that every time we were forming up into teams we would be reorganized. We tended to meet any new situation by reorganizing, and a wonderful method it can be for creating the illusion of progress while producing confusion, inefficiency, and demoralization." So wrote the Roman Petronius—in 210 B.C.

Warming a chair, going through the motions—or wearing a pair of golden handcuffs—is no way to go about laboring, much less living. As Eugene O'Neill wrote:

A man's work is in danger of deteriorating
when he thinks he has found the one best formula for doing it. If he thinks that he is likely
to feel that, all he needs is merely to go repeat-
ing himself. So long as a person is searching for
better ways of doing his work, he is fairly safe.

Some people have exquisite antennae that help
them sense both organizational and personal signals
that tell them it's time to let go and move on.

When an organization starts to lack vision and
fails to acknowledge the problem or, to cite Charlie
Brown, takes this position: "If you don't know where
you're going, any road will take you there," then may
be time to move on. Such companies lose their direction because they fail to remember their destination."

Some leave when a company closes its eyes to a
sliding market share, increased competition, or
changing market conditions—or when top executives
choose to blame deteriorating conditions on vaguely
articulated external factors.

Others go when the company becomes opaque to
fresh ideas, or when it gets caught up in its own success and fails to recognize that nothing recedes like
success, then it's time to move on.

And when one's career path is repeatedly
blocked—or when work no longer carries with it
meaning, value, and excitement—then it may be time
to move on.

And most important, it's time to move on if you
feel you're being treated like a cormorant.

A fisherman says to the cormorant, "Go get me a fish." The bird flies off and returns with a large fish in its beak. The fisherman strokes the bird, offers warm words of praise and congratulations, and then says, "Go get me another fish." Off the bird flies again, soon to return with its prey. The bird is well trained, loyal, and appears indefatigable.

By the end of the day the bird has worked its tail off but has gotten no reward other than kind words and strokes on the back. The cormorant is not free to enjoy its success—because the fisherman has placed a tight metal ring around its neck, and if it ever tries to swallow even the smallest fish, it will choke to death.

The lesson is clear: work hard—but never let the job strangle you. And enjoy the fruits of your labor.

Overwork without pacing has been a problem since long before the invention of the beeper, the pager, and the cell phone—devices that allow work to chase us even to the beaches and the mountains.

We all must learn to give work a rest — to set aside inviolate time for our personal needs. Otherwise we run the risk of ending up like the The Man with the Hoe as described by the poet Edwin Markham in 1899:

> Bowed by the weight of centuries he leans
> Upon his hoe and gazes on the ground,
> The emptiness of ages in his face,
> And on his back the burden of the world.

And we must never, ever be afraid to take risks and move.

The key to happiness in the modern working world is amassing a skill set broad enough that you can take your work with you wherever you move. It's important to develop a sense of "concerned detachment"—being invested in what you do but at the same time somewhat removed and objective. Time, talent, conviction, focus, and intellectual capital will be the critical resources of the future. One third as many people will be doing three times as much work as we do today, with greater leverage in the markets and at a faster rate. That means we must have the courage to take risks, make mistakes, and bounce back from failure. "Mishaps are like knives that either serve us or cut us," Melville wrote, "as we grasp them by the blade or the handle."

We need to tell our children that—since they will be the ones entering that new workforce. And we must also pass on the words of investor Theodore Forstmann: "In a state-run society the government promises you security, thereby creating the illusion that the opposite of security is breaking molds and taking risks. In fact, the opposite of security is not risk; the opposite of security is insecurity; and the only way to overcome insecurity is to take risks."

In the play *I'm Not Rappaport*, there's a wonderful exchange between two men in their eighties sitting on a park bench, eying a group of adolescents:

"They don't like us."
"Why not? We haven't done anything to them."

"That's not important. What is important is that
we represent their coming attractions."

If we look defeated and detached in our older
years, we'll come off as features to be avoided; but if
we stay relevant, share our wisdom and engage our
juniors, we'll be perceived as must-see double bills.

It all depends on how we react when the unwelcome visitor of aging time becomes a permanent guest
at the table at work. Contempt and resentments
sometimes flare, along with jealousies and a sense that
the younger generation just can't wait for the old
guard to pack it in.

Perceptive people understand how important it is
to pass the intergenerational baton in both directions—that we should court older friends when
young, and younger colleagues when we grow old.

Many seasoned workers feel they've paid their
dues and that it's time for others to pay them homage.
That's a bankrupt strategy that isolates people. Many
experience a low-lying depression while looking back
at unfulfilled dreams of "what if"—while looking forward to a life of uncertainty.

We need to keep growing, exploring, and grabbing
opportunites. Pablo Picasso had it right. "I've spent
my whole life," he said, on turning ninety, "learning
how to become a child."

⎯⎯❦❦⎯⎯

Above all we need to bear in mind that work
remains at the center a spiritual commodity. The way

we feel about the work we do influences how we feel about ourselves and our families, how we feel about our futures and our children's futures, and how we feel about life itself. We need to pass that on to our children, along with the words of social psychologist Carol Tavis:

> Happiness lies not in mindless hedonism, but in mindful challenge; not in having unlimited opportunities but in focused possibilities; not in self-absorption, but in absorption of the world; not in having it done for you but in doing it yourself. The unexamined life may not be worth living, but the unlived life is not worth examining.

Rapid change in the world of work will be a given. This is a time, in T. S. Eliot's words, for decisions and revisions which a minute will reverse. We can try to influence what happens. We can sit on the sidelines and watch things happen. We can stop things from happening. Or we can be in the position of always asking "What happened?"

To a large degree that choice is ours.

5

LAUGHING AND LAMENTING

To laugh is to risk appearing a fool.
To weep is to risk appearing sentimental.
To risk for another is to risk involvement.
To expose feelings is to risk rejection.
To place your dreams before the crowd is to risk
    ridicule.
To love is to risk not being loved in return.
To go forward in the face of overwhelming odds
    is to risk failure.
But risks must be taken because the greatest risk
    is to risk nothing.
People who risk nothing, do nothing, have
    nothing, are nothing.
They may avoid suffering and sorrow, but they
    cannot learn, feel, grow, or love.
Chained by their uncertainties, they are slaves.
They have forfeited their freedom.
Only people who take risks are free.
                      —*Author unknown*

"What Does a Pizza Look Like When It's Alive?"

Jeff was a special neighbor, a precocious five-year-old who used to show up in our kitchen conveniently at dinnertime in search of good cookies or just a chance to mix it up.

One night he arrived just as we were about to have something to eat. We asked him to join us, and he happily accepted the invitation.

After sitting down at the table, he looked at his plate and asked, "Uncle Barrie, what did this look like when it was alive?"

"What?" I asked, stunned. "When what was alive?" We were eating a pizza and a salad.

"When the pizza was alive," he said. We all laughed. An old Quaker saying sprang to my mind as the laughter died down and we sat around the table looking at each other in sheepish silence: "Don't speak unless you can improve upon the silence." But I had to answer the question. It had been asked with all the naïveté of a child, but with an earnestness and curiosity so compelling that the question required an intelligent response. Composing my thoughts, I asked, "What made you think the pizza was once alive?"

His mother, he said, had told him that everything we eat was once alive. Meat comes from animals. Fruit comes from trees, and vegetables grow in the ground. So where does a pizza come from? An animal, the ground, or a tree? His thinking was perfectly logical if you follow the original formula.

I told him that all the parts of the pizza—the dough, tomatoes, cheese, pepperoni, and mushrooms—were once alive and that the pizza was a mixture of a whole bunch of things put together. It was like a family—brothers, sisters, parents, aunts, and uncles. Or, I added, like when a bunch of companies get together and decide to form one big company (his father was an investment banker, so I thought I might be striking a chord somewhere). Still, I marveled at his comments, and at his insight.

I've never looked at a pizza the same way since. A five-year-old's question made me think about the shortcuts I take and the assumptions I make that deprive me of valuable insights.

I see a pizza now and think about laughing at someone else's expense, and about how the incident brought out a wide range of emotions in me: love for a special boy; laughter, because the question really was funny; guilt and shame, because I had judged prematurely; pleasure and excitement, because I had made the metaphorical connection to a conglomerate. (Jeff's father called me later that night to remonstrate and laughingly asked me what was I trying to do, raise another capitalist?)

Pizza, because of Jeff, has become for me a

metaphor for all the tangled and intersecting emotions that coexist within our living souls—love and fear, contempt and sadness, tenderness and laughter, frustration and rage, jealousy and hurt, guilt and terror, disgust and shame, pleasure and pain, remorse and fulfillment, passion and boredom. All those emotions sit right there inside us and play with and against each other.

How often a laugh becomes a convenient way of not dealing with something we fear. How often a funny, offbeat comment can open up a whole series of insights about the concern of intimacy or deep prejudice. How often a quick quip lets us deal with things we resent, disdain, or want no part of.

Feelings mean a lot. For some, they matter more than thought or action, and I've worked with many people who would rather "go with their gut" than trust any traditional "head" logic.

I've been privy to a number of "rational" decisions that were in fact governed by highly emotional determinates. But they were "sold" by using the best "corporate logic." A case in point: The CEO wanted to move his company headquarters from Manhattan to the suburbs. His rationale was based on an extensive cost/benefit analysis that proved the move would save large sums of money. The reality was that the CEO didn't like the long commute into town and wanted to move the company closer to his home. In no way did he fool the troops. They acquiesced because they had no choice. But he clearly lost leadership points.

Our reservoir of feelings is deep and wide. They bring a necessary vitality to the way we think or act. Soft or touchy-feely emotions can be just as important as hard data. Ask seasoned people in the business world and they will tell you that not being aware of emotions puts you at a competitive disadvantage when you're sitting on one side of a negotiating table. Herb Simon, the Nobel Prize–winning professor of computer science argues cogently that we have to be in touch with the rational (logical), the nonrational (intuitive), and the irrational (emotional) in order to enhance our judgment and decision-making powers.

The gifted teacher, etymologist (and poker enthusiast) Richard Lederer has pointed out that while an IBM mainframe computer can beat the world champion in chess, it could never do the same thing in poker.

Chess involves long-term strategy. To win you need to think two or three moves ahead of where you are at any given moment. In chess everything's out in the open. In poker, nothing is obvious. To win at poker you need to remember the look on your opponent's face when he drew to a full house three hands ago—or three weeks ago. You also need to learn how to hide your feelings and bluff—to hide the utter despair in your heart that you're betting the farm on a pair of deuces. A computer can't compute or read feelings—and therefore can't beat the best poker players in the world at five-card draw or seven-card stud.

Feelings often appear "out of the blue" and "for no apparent reason" because their roots are deep and invested in happenings that are burned into our psyches at pivotal points in our lives. The more we are tuned in to them, the less vulnerable we become.

The Pygmy people of Central Africa believe that man has seven senses, not five. The sixth sense is emotion, and the seventh, which not everybody possesses, is the ability to heal.

They have a point. Emotions can and do heal. But they can also hurt and cause severe damage. As John Milton put it: "The mind is its own place, and in itself can make a heaven of hell and a hell of heaven." Laughing and lamenting restore our souls as we move through life. We need to let our inheritors know about those restorative powers, just as we have learned about them from our forebears.

Diagnosed with a fatal disease, the editor Norman Cousins made a basic decision to use humor, and particularly laughter, as a weapon against his body's unwelcome invaders. He watched a ton of funny movies and read humorous books. Not only was he able to stem the tide of his disease, but he also achieved spectacular results. He lived many years beyond the time when his doctors said he would die, and in effect had the last laugh on them.

His laughter, along with the other treatments, may have stimulated his immune system. The body's natural defenses kicked in and attacked the toxins in his body. Was it laughter alone that had a therapeutic effect? No. But his ability to take charge and not lose control, his sense of hope, and his fight against capitulation worked along with the medicines. Cousins's humor, optimism, and ability to innovate converted his hell into a heaven.

Laughter in the face of *adversity* simply has a restorative effect.

The humorist Sam Levenson told this story: "My folks were immigrants escaping the prejudices of war-torn Europe. They fell under the spell of the American Dream that the streets were paved with gold. When Pop got here he found out three things: the streets were not paved with gold; the streets were not even paved; and he was supposed to do the paving." A perfect example demonstrating Reinhold Niebuhr's point that "laughter is a kind of no man's land between faith and despair."

Humor can be seen as a violation of expectation. Following surgery for a hip replacement, an elderly man left the recovery room in obvious and great pain.

"How are you doing?" his son asked solicitously.

"I can't kick," his father replied—and then laughed like crazy watching the bemused reaction of his son while neutralizing the sting of the surgery.

While playing tennis, a man with severe gut problems and chronic diarrhea suffered a detached retina when his opponent smashed a net shot into his left eye. "I don't know whether to shit or go blind," he said to friends as he waited for surgery; the humor buffered his fear of losing his sight.

A friend has an annual sculpture party at his summer home in August to which guests are invited to bring their "works." Last year one work brilliantly captured the message. A woman's pink silk slip was draped over a tree trunk with an ax embedded in it. The sculptor was letting everyone know he'd just lost his job.

Laughter makes a feared enemy a friend. Jimmy Durante poked fun at his nose. Rodney Dangerfield complained, "I don't get no respect." Jackie Gleason, as Ralph Kramden, covered up his low self-esteem by being a know-it-all. And obviously he touched a chord: A group in New York called the Royal Association for the Longevity and Preservation of the Honeymooners (RALPH) still meets regularly.

George Burns used to say that at his age—ninety-eight—he couldn't afford to buy green bananas. "Make sure you go to other people's funerals," Yogi Berra advised. "Otherwise they might not come to yours." And "when you get to the fork in the road," he also said, "take it."

A colleague who consults with businesses recounted how he sat through a dreadful staff meeting. The CEO of the company went into a long harangue: The world is divided into two groups of people, those who lead and those who get out of the way and follow. The job of the people in that room was to lead, and damn them all if they didn't get out and bust their butts.

The CEO turned on his heel authoritatively and

left, turning the meeting over to my consultant friend.

"So what do you think?"

Everyone in the room was very uncomfortable. A long silence ensued. Then a senior manager raised his hand. "I think the world is divided into two groups of people," he said. "Those who divide the world into two groups and those who don't."

The room dissolved into laughter, dispelling a painful atmosphere.

An editor related his experience of how his entire newsroom came down with a debilitating case of writer's block. It was a stuffy July night, the air-conditioning had been shut off by the penurious building management, and no one could concentrate on the tasks at hand. Deadlines were fast approaching, and the editor had to do something to unblock the staff or the paper would never come out.

He walked into the newsroom, drew up a chair beside a group of writers, and asked, "So, who do you think has the better vocal range, Whitney Houston or Roy Orbison?"

Within five minutes the entire newsroom was embroiled in an utterly absurd argument over the issue. Writers stood on their desks singing "I Will Always Love You," "Pretty Woman," and "Only the Lonely," with the women struggling horribly for Orbison's bass notes and the men making idiots of themselves as they tried for Houston's highest soprano. Within an hour after the laughter had died down, the editor had all the copy he could handle, and the writers all went home, still smiling.

Time spent laughing, the ancients used to say, is time spent with the gods. Laughter helps us feel better not only for physiological reasons but for psychological ones as well. We laugh at Yogi Berra, George Burns, and the manager who dared blow holes in the "world is divided" paradigm because they poke fun at the traditional platitudes and poke holes in the overinflated. They tell the truth, and the truth is often funny.

Humor is the great leveler—and it's absolutely no accident that Athens, the birthplace of democracy, was also the birthplace of comedy. The absurdity of humorous Greek plays—or aphorisms—could flourish only in an open society, where telling the truth, even as a form of political dissent, was encouraged.

Think for a minute about what we laugh at: sensitive issues like death, religion, politics, sex, aging, disease, disfigurement, mishaps, race, family tragedy—things that make us uneasy to contemplate seriously so we make light of them. Laughter takes the hurt away and detoxifies the painful.

Art Buchwald explained it this way: "People ask what I'm trying to do with humor. I'm getting even. I'm constantly avenging hurts from the past." This from a man who spent his childhood in orphanages and then graduated to the Marines during the Second World War, where he saw enough pain to last a lifetime. His humor is a weapon, sharply honed, and designed to sting—to take away bites from the past.

Oppressed groups joke about themselves and their oppressors, as in the saying "When the enemy falls, don't rejoice: but don't pick him up either."

For some, humor is a tool to ward off fears of technology and "progress." How else to explain the following:

The word has come down from the Dean
That by way of the teaching machine
King Oedipus Rex
Could have learned about sex
Without ever touching the Queen.

And only certain types of humor can make a point that hits home. Imagine, for example, if a consulting firm did a cost/benefit analysis of the local symphony, a horrific scenario that was first dreamed up in 1954:

The four oboe players have nothing to do for long periods of time, so their number should be reduced. Likewise the brass and tympany sections. All the first violins play identical notes: unnecessary duplication; cut there, too. If volume is required, an electronic amplifier can be brought in.

There is too much repetition of some musical passages, so scores should be drastically pruned.

No useful purpose can be served by having the horns repeat a passage that has just been played by the strings; if redundant passages are eliminated, total concert time can be reduced from two hours to 20 minutes. That will save on the lighting bill.

In the unlikely event these changes lead to some falling off in attendance, close off sections of the auditorium with a consequential savings in overhead expense in such areas as usher salaries. . . .

We laugh—because it could happen.

Nothing can be as powerful as the humorous barb. "Wilt thou show the whole wealth of thy wit in an instant?" Shakespeare asks in *The Merchant of Venice*. Dorothy Parker, in reviewing an actor's performance, said it was the worst she had ever seen. A year later she dismissed the same actor with the comment, "He wasn't up to his usual standard."

And sometimes a sense of humor may actually help foster longevity. A while ago, a group of Boston doctors went to interview a group of centenarians in South America. One woman they talked to professed to be 114 years old. She smoked a pipe, took a nip every day, and ate no yogurt. When asked the secret of her longevity, she simply replied: "I don't know. Maybe I just like it around here."

Obviously genes and a number of other factors had an influence on her longevity. But her "attitude"—just smiling and liking it there—surely had to have helped her live so long.

We need to tell our children that.

Laughing and humor occupy only a small part of the emotional spectrum. There is too much tragedy in this world to laugh it all away. The Holocaust, the Gulag, and the Killing Fields still haunt many of us.

Mental hospitals are full of people fighting off demons they can't control. A host of debilitating illnesses compromise the talents and dampen the dreams of millions of people every day. Others search for political freedom while depressingly large numbers try to scrape together food for their children.

It's a paradox: in a land where we own more than ever before, many feel more deprived. Where we make more use than ever of labor-saving devices, many feel increasingly harried and unable to relax. In a country where more people than ever remain eager to stuff insights into other people's minds, many feel under greater stress. While technology instantly puts facts at our fingertips, we feel less secure in making decisions. In a computer-connected society, many feel more disconnected.

We all experience inner pain to a degree, and how we deal with that pain—acknowledge it or seek to avoid it—has a direct impact on our lives.

Some tackle the hurt on their own. Some find it helps to talk with a trusted friend or seek professional help. Still others deny the pain or hope that it will simply go away. But hurts never entirely disappear. If they remain unexpressed, they can fester like a bad wound and grow to become the gangrene of the soul.

At the suggestion of a colleague, I saw a twenty-five-year-old woman with Down's Syndrome one January.

Until a couple of weeks before our meeting, Charlotte had been a very happy person who did all the household chores with a good degree of gusto. But she had become acutely angry, suspicious, and hard to handle. She lost her temper easily and feared going to bed and being alone.

With the help of her parents and her sister, over a number of weeks, we put together the pieces of a wrenching and painful puzzle.

It turned out that Charlotte was watching TV while vacuuming one afternoon and caught a public service announcement having to do with people like her. The message in the announcement was loud and clear: Do Not Send These People Away. Love Them and Keep Them at Home.

Even though no one had even hinted at Charlotte's having to leave home, the message disturbed her deeply. She was terrified, but she said nothing.

A few weeks later, Christmas arrived and the family gave Charlotte a special gift to celebrate a surprise vacation they would all be taking soon—her own set of luggage!

Charlotte immediately assumed she was being sent away.

Over time, lots of love and support resolved the situation. But the episode only drove home to me how we owe it to ourselves to express our pain—and of how easy it is to make innocent assumptions.

⤙⟋⟍⤚

A woman I know gave birth to a beautiful baby girl. Everything appeared fine until the dreadful day when she realized her daughter was deaf.

A huge range of emotions engulfed her—fear, anger, resentment, hurt, embarrassment, panic, failure, and guilt.

But Karen had the innate wisdom to give vent to her emotions. She expressed her fear and her panic. She shared her feelings of embarrassment and guilt and failure with her friends.

"I learned that handicaps are not synonymous with limitations and that our daughter could learn, love, and relate to others if we felt good about her," she said to me. "I guess you learn to cope with whatever you're given. I don't believe that God could make a child suffer this way. I never thought I'd laugh again. I thought I'd never plan for the future. I've learned to cry with people and not be ashamed of my honest emotions. The more our daughter grows, the more we grow with her." Understanding feelings and putting them in proper perspective gives us a better sense of control. It makes us less like Alice in Wonderland, who lamented, "I wish I hadn't cried so much. I shall be punished for it now, I suppose, by being drowned in my own tears."

⤙⟋⟍⤚

In his treatise on ethics, Aristotle explained his understanding of anger.

"Anyone can be angry," he wrote. "That is easy.

But to be angry with the right person, to the right degree, at the right time, for the right purpose, and in the right way, that is not easy."

A woman who came to see me had enjoyed an impressive college career, was married, and had raised three children. Deciding she wanted to go back to work, she quickly found she lacked credentials. She was advised to return to school, which she did. But after she earned an advanced degree she was told she lacked experience. She was furious; she reminded me of Ty Cobb, who, it was said, was so tempestuous a character he would climb a mountain to punch an echo.

I suggested that the woman try a little corporate alchemy by taking out an ad in the local paper and describing herself in business terms. She did so charmingly:

> Situation wanted: 40-year-old CEO of a small but diversified company. Salary 40–60 k/year. Has served as director of purchasing, product development, and marketing. Expertise in finance, budgets, control, planning, and forecasting as well as organizational development. Used to making tough decisions. Best in crisis. Good health, energetic, good appearance. No absentee record. Company has been consistently profitable, with no major debts. Expansion at this point limited, seeking new ventures.

By converting her academic and domestic skills into corporate language, she channeled her anger in the right way—and she got a job. She learned that anger is one letter short of danger.

Anger left unexpressed, though, can contribute to one of the most debilitating and little-understood illnesses of our time: depression, which some believe is anger turned inward.

Depression is more than what Somerset Maugham described as the "slough of despond." It can be utter mental paralysis. Depression is the mind moving through molasses—where everything hurts and where all the days are filled with nights. It is what Jean-Paul Sartre called "huis clos"— "no exit."

At one point I worked with a young man in a depression so deep he could not even imagine the notion of relief. I asked him to imagine it was a cold day in January, and that his bladder was so full it was going to burst, and that he had finally found a place to pee. Would the release, the final emptying, the long and luxuriant pee, bring him pleasure and relief? I asked. "No," he said. The response in itself was diagnostic.

Depression is not just an isolated emotion. It influences all parts of our bodies. As William Harvey, who first described the circulation of blood, put it in the seventeenth century: "Every affection of the mind that is attended with either pain or pleasure, hope or fear is the cause of agitation, whose influence extends to the heart." And, I might add, to other parts of the body as well.

Medication helps. Loving friends and families help, too. Most important is an understanding that depression is far, far, different from moral weakness.

We are not always responsible for what happens to us, and we need to appreciate that.

No group is immune from depression: newborns, children, adolescents, adults, and the elderly all struggle with it. Socioeconomic status, talent, or a happy childhood do not vaccinate us against the dark genes, neurotransmitters, and life experiences that bear on the situation. We are products of nature and nurture, and while we are not doomed by our genes, neither are we passive passengers just waiting for a biochemical time bomb to go off. We can influence, to a large degree, what happens to us.

⤜ ☙ ❧ ⤛

A colleague shared with a me a letter sent him by an engineer.

Henry couldn't understand what was happening to him. He had a loving family, a good job, wonderful friends, and a firm belief in God. He assumed, he said, that his problem was not mental but moral.

He lived without hope and felt, in his own eyes, worthless. He feared crowds and was afraid to go outside, but he couldn't figure out what had caused his great affliction.

"I am not a weeper," Henry said. "But I cried a hell of a lot in those terrible days. I've had some serious and painful surgery in the past, and I'd be willing to endure those procedures again rather than go through another depression. I always thought 'nervous breakdowns' happen only to unstable, weak, people—and I'd never considered myself such.

"Initially I was too embarrassed to get some help. I'm from the school that says that you take care of emotional problems on your own. But the pain overwhelmed me, and I had no other choice. It was the right thing. The combination of my belief in the Almighty, a caring doctor, family support, and medication got me over the hump." This was a cry from the heart. And because Henry found the strength and the courage to lament—to speak his pain out loud, to share his hurt with close friends, and do something about it—he found a degree of relief.

———⌒⌒———

A man I know sank into a deep depression while undergoing chemotherapy treatments.

His depression hit him at a time when the news on the treatment front was pretty good. His tumors were shrinking. But his head, as he put it, simply shut down one day. He felt nothing. He sensed nothing. He stared into space.

Luckily, Frank had a very good oncology nurse, and he confided his hopelessness to her.

She arrived at an immediate and correct diagnosis: his mind had simply come to a halt because it was terrified of what would happen if the good news turned bad. Bad news would mean the chemotherapy wasn't working—and that would mean the need for radical and disfiguring surgery.

He couldn't deal with that possibility so he erected a psychic sign: Going out of Business. All

Items Marked Down. Please Bring Your Vehicle to the Loading Dock.

A therapist told Frank to bombard his five senses with good things so he could begin to feel again. With the return of feeling, the depression would begin to lift. In the construct of the Pygmies of Central Africa, stimulating feelings through the five traditional senses would help to bring back the sixth sense, emotion, and then lead to the seventh, healing. The therapist's suggestions:

Play soothing music and a bit of Vivaldi, Bach, and Telemann.

Buy the sweetest, pulpiest orange juice you can find and enjoy it with the most obscene breakfast you've ever imagined. Spare no sausage.

Go to the florist and get some sweet-smelling flowers.

Go for a walk and enjoy the freedom of movement and the beauty of a cold December New England landscape. Enjoy the sunset. Watch the vapor escape from your mouth and capture that crinkly feeling when your mustache freezes, and the weird tickle when it melts after you've gone back indoors.

Make a fire in the woodstove and sit next to it to absorb the warmth and the smell that wood makes when it burns very hot.

Put a kettle on the stove and fill it with water and a few sticks of raw cinnamon bark. Go outside for a second and come back in to smell that vivid, almost red, scent.

Baby the senses. Feelings will come back and will trigger the memory of emotions. The depression will lift as emotions begin their return and the healing will begin.

Frank did as the therapist suggested and his depression lifted in a matter of days.

———∽ ∾———

"If depression had no termination, then suicide would indeed be the only remedy," wrote the novelist William Styron, who himself suffers from depression. "But one need not sound a false or insincere note to stress the truth that depression is not the soul's annihilation. Men and women who have recovered from the disease, and there are countless, bear witness to what is the disease's only saving grace, that it is conquerable." In lamentation, as in laughter, we overcome. That is wisdom we have received from our forebears and we need to give to those who follow us. As Goethe said: "He only learns his freedom and existence who daily conquers them anew."

The sum total of ourselves is always the product of a struggle. The end result always looks easy, but no one's life is as easy as it seems. We all have our crosses to bear. We have all been nicked. Positive feelings provide the energy and the courage to explore, while negative emotions reduce our self-confidence and limit our choices. We carry both sets of emotions inside us—parts of the pizza. In the end this means we realize certain insights and achievements only during moments of pain. As Nietzsche said, "A gem cannot be polished without friction, nor man perfected without trials."

We are and remain imperfect. Feelings lend music to our words that make them alternately harmonious or discordant. Emotions give us a dimension larger than our physical presence and make us more approachable and less toxic to ourselves and to others (or less approachable and more toxic). "What is man that Thou art mindful of him?" Emerson asked. The emotions play a large part in answering that question.

We need to periodically do childlike things—free of scrutiny or judgment—and slip free of "being mature" or "grown up" all the time. We can let go. As Peter Pan said, "I never hope that it would be/Beneath my dignity/To climb a tree."

We need to tell our children that, but also that it's OK to cry and laugh and scream, that it's good to be passionate about a cause or resonate empathically with the downtrodden or experience a special oneness with a person we love. These are emotions that connect us to ourselves and to others.

We are an abstract painting of vibrant colors, painted on life's canvas, which constantly changes. We need to pay attention to those feelings, look at the colors and respond accordingly.

Nikos Kazantzakis got at those feelings at a cellular level when he wrote, in Zorba the Greek, "What a strange machine man is! You fill him with bread, wine, fish, and radishes, and out of him comes sighs, laughter, and dreams."

And that is what gives us our uniqueness, our essence of being human. That is what we have received from our forebears. That is what we pass on to those who matter.

6

LINKING

Oh the comfort, the inexpressible comfort, of
    feeling safe with a person.
Having neither to weigh thoughts or measure
    words.
But pour them all out, just as they are chaff
    and grain together,
Knowing that a faithful hand will take and sift
    them what is worth keeping,
And then, with the breath of kindness, blow
    them away.

—*George Eliot*

"Do You Mind Cleaning Up Crap?"

A number of years ago one of our children became seriously ill and faced difficult surgery. We were worried sick and scared to death. Friends from various parts of the country called to offer encouragement and advice.

One afternoon the phone rang, and it was a psychiatrist colleague from San Francisco who also happened to be a Jesuit priest. After we exchanged initial greetings and he offered his sympathy and support, Gene asked if it would be all right with us if he said a novena, nine consecutive days of prayer under the rights of the Roman Catholic church, for our son.

I was so moved that I literally could not speak. Gene knew very well that I was Jewish. But he also knew I felt deeply that there was only one God, and that there are many paths by which to approach Him.

I regained my composure after a minute and, with tears in my eyes, I asked him to pray especially hard for our boy.

Twenty-five years later and with our son totally recovered, I can never think of his illness, the surgery, and the subsequent recovery without linking with Gene, and the power of his presence and caring.

The world connects not by molecules. It connects through ideas, hopes, faces, dreams, actions, stories, and memories.

It connects through music and sound, through images and words, through common tastes and smells, and through cries of pain and joy and powerful symbols. God gave us memories so we could all smell roses in December. That's a link we all share.

Individually we represent connected voices, all crying out from a number of different arenas and times for essentially the same things. Even if we do not speak the same language or share the same religion or culture, we connect to each other. For thousands of years, at the very least, we've had common dreams of a full belly, a warm place to sleep in the winter, and shelter when it rains.

Yet there is as much diversity in our connections as there are different ways of measuring happiness. Charles de Gaulle lamented that it was close to impossible to govern a country that produces over forty kinds of cheese. Yet *La Belle France* has proved governable because some common idea of "Frenchness" unites the country.

We connect throughout the centuries—from the paintings in the cave at Altamira to today's newspaper. We can identify with the stories laid out in *Don Quixote, The Great Gatsby, Death Be Not Proud,* and *Bonfire of the Vanities*—because we've either experienced those same people ourselves or because we know people who have.

During the summer one of the most pastoral places on the East Coast is Tanglewood, nestled in the rolling Berkshire hills of western Massachusetts. You can take a picnic, sit out on the broad sloping lawn, admire the colors of the landscape, and listen to some of the most beautiful music in the world, performed by the Boston Symphony Orchestra. One night as a concert was about to begin, I was leafing through the program notes and was bowled over by the diversity. A Japanese violinist was playing a Russian violin concerto with an American orchestra composed of musicians from all over the world, all under the direction of a German conductor, and playing before a United Nations audience. They were all inextricably linked toward a common goal—to be the best. That linkage—of nature, the genius of the composer, the talent of his interpreters, and the presence of a receptive audience—gave new meaning to the words *connection* and *synergy*.

How we link—and with whom and for how long and why—defines the essence of our being. Linking is both a celebration of our diversity and an affirmation of it.

That's an important message to pass down to our inheritors—along with this vital point: all of us are the result of a linking, of the simple connection between the egg and the sperm. We begin by connecting. And we never stop. As Sandy McPherson wrote in her poem "Pregnancy," "Some day your seed will run back to hug you."

Some linkages are short and intense, while others survive generations. Some defy traditional logic and remain cloaked in mystery. Families separated from each other for years because of conflict suddenly unite. Countries that once tried to put each other out of existence become major trading partners. Competitors out to sink each other form joint ventures.

Our inner world is a stage without boundaries in the theater of the mind. On it, we play different roles where past, present, and future events merge. Opposites exist comfortably, and uncomfortably, side by side, and parts of things equal wholes. It's an internal superhighway, our crossroads leading to remarkable destinations.

The most important link we forge in our lives is with our own selves. This may sound obvious, but some people can, and others cannot, make that link.

A father of a young boy told me a story about his son, who, though eight, still sucked his thumb.

The boy and his thumb were inseparable. On a number of occasions, the father berated the son, saying, "Stop sucking your thumb. You look like a baby," or "You'll get buck teeth," or "People will make fun of you." (The father had sucked his thumb as a child and had needed braces.)

One day the boy was totally involved with his thumb, and when the father launched into his standard monologue, the son stopped him. "Daddy," he said. "I suck my thumb because that's me."

To the father's credit, he did not interrupt this connection. His boy was linking with himself, reveling in the exquisite joy of instant gratification. Insert thumb; get pleasure. He was there! And nothing could substitute at that moment for the sheer pleasure of that thumb.

How we appear and relate to our bodies may serve as a defense for underlying concerns.

A man called me years ago, saying he couldn't come to grips with his son's appearance. It wasn't so much his clothes, the father said, but his hair. "It's long and scraggly. And to be truthful, it embarrasses the hell out of me. I don't like to be seen with him, and he looks like a girl."

My office is in Harvard Square, the capital of Anything Goes, USA, 02138, and I've seen long hair here for as long as I've been in Cambridge. I asked the father what he expected me to do.

"Just talk to the boy," he said, "and see if you can get him to cut his hair." I said I would see him if the son made the appointment personally. But, I added, I wanted to make it clear at the outset: I wasn't a barber, and I would not ask the boy to get his hair cut. His son, whose name was Sean, did make the appointment and showed up looking no different from any other student I'd seen around the Square. He stood tall and slender and spoke in a soft voice, forcing me to move forward and strain to catch his words. He told me of the pressure he'd gotten from his father and about the resentment he continued to feel over the issue of hair.

He complained about the constant mantra "Cut your hair." But as he spoke I noticed a curious thing.

He pulled his hair down with his thumb and index finger, brought it to the front of his face, rolled it between those two fingers, and stared at it contemplatively.

After watching this and listening to him, I said, "Look, I don't care how long your hair is. That's your business. But I'm curious as to why you keep it long."

Sean stopped his ritual and said that no one had ever asked him that before. All anybody had said was "Cut your hair."

Then Sean paused for a second. "You probably didn't notice," he said, "but I bring my hair to the front of my face and look at it." He paused again. "Because if I don't look at my hair, I'm afraid I'm going to disappear."

I'm sure I winced, and I know I felt a chill run up my spine. The hairs on my back froze as I realized this young man had the most fragile hold on reality I'd ever encountered. Only a few strands of hair separated him from being and vanishing.

Sean deeply needed help—not someone to bully or shame him or make superficial assumptions. Those moves would only precipitate a major breakdown. He needed to link with himself. Badly.

Sean eventually was hospitalized. But the episode got me thinking. People are often more fragile than we think. And people are also often less fragile than we think. But the trouble is, you never know which is which. So tread lightly. You never know when someone may be having trouble linking inside or externally—and we should never act or judge others too quickly because we feel uncomfortable. That's a legacy worth passing on.

<hr />

Martin Luther King Jr. said that we connect with others "in an inescapable network of mutuality, woven into a common garment of destiny."

How we do that is nothing short of a miracle, considering how different and incongruous our relationships appear to be. Pete Seeger's song *"Somos El Barco"* sums it up nicely:

> The stream sings it to the river, the river sings it to
> the sea.
> The sea sings it to the boat that carries you and me.
> The boat we are sailing on was built by many
> hands,
> The sea we are sailing on touches every sand.
> We are the boat, we are the sea.
> I sail in you. You sail in me.

Some linkages are intimate and intense: those of family and lovers, or soldiers in battle, or teammates in a game, or choir members, or prisoners; others are distant and utilitarian and "strictly business," like heavy users of the Internet—close but not too close. Still others are like porcupines on a cold day, when they move close to stay warm, but not too close for fear of sticking each other—an approach/avoidance game. There is, after all, an optimal intimacy and distance necessary between people.

And some linkages simply recall George Gershwin's words about Ginger Rogers: "She had a little love for everybody, but not very much for anybody."

For a period of time, my neighbor and I did not acknowledge each other's existence. I felt that he had seriously overstepped the bounds of propriety on more than one occasion, and he must have felt the same way about me. We had erected what some call the "Devil's Walk." That's when two farmers can't agree on a common boundary line, so they throw up two sets of fences—each on clearly undisputed land. And the area between the fences is open only to the devil.

One day I saw my neighbor putting out his garbage, and I felt the need to take the higher road. I went over and apologized for anything I might have done. Obviously touched, he came over and hugged me. He said he was sorry for anything he had done, too. As time went on, while we never became best friends, we were at least civil to one another. We linked—like porcupines on a cold day—but at least we were able to end the standoff, form a connection, and get rid of the Devil's Walk between us.

A Boston businessman collapsed while on a trip to New York. A combination of overwork, stress, and a terrible diet had taken its toll, and he was rushed by ambulance to the nearest hospital, which wasn't in exactly the best part of town. He eventually found himself sharing a room with a man from the opposite end of the socioeconomic spectrum. You could not have found two more different people to share one room. Yet as they lay there in their beds, they formed a connection. Each shared a great fear over his individual medical condition. Somehow, they figured out that they could help each other.

"You pray for me and I'll pray for you," the Boston businessman said. "That way we'll double our message." And the strategy worked. They linked prayers and prevailed.

─❧❧─

There is a wonderful parable in which God shows a man the difference between Heaven and Hell.

God leads the man into a room in Hell. A group of people sit around a pot of stew. Everyone is famished—yet curiously, each one holds a very long spoon. There's the rub: the spoons are long enough to reach the pot, but too long to accommodate the mechanics of getting the contents to their own mouths without spilling the stew out of the spoons.

"Come now," God tells the man. "I'll show you Heaven." They enter another room—and it's exactly the same scene: a group of people sitting around a pot of stew with long spoons. But these people are fed and contented.

"I don't understand," says the man. "The two rooms are identical."

"Ah," says God. "Don't you see? In the second room they have learned to feed each other." That is linking. Strong relationships may be made in heaven, but they need to be managed on earth. That takes commitment, sharing, and tolerance—and a host of refueling techniques.

A grandfather, father, and son lived in a small house together. Money was scarce, and when the grandfather took ill, he became a terrible burden to the father.

The father approached the son and gave him a blanket. "Take your grandfather to the barn," he said, "so that he may live out his remaining days there."

The boy protested, saying it was lonely and cold in the barn and that the grandfather would surely die if left out there alone. Where was his father's compassion?

The father told the boy to do as he was told, and so he took his grandfather to the barn, though the boy felt torn and humiliated to banish him to such an isolated place.

A short time later, the father spied the son returning alone from the barn—with half a blanket.

"What are you doing with half a blanket?" he asked. "I told you to give the blanket to your grandfather."

"One half is for grandfather," the boy replied. "The other half is for you when you get old and I take you to the barn."

How we treat others may have an impact on how others treat us. Caring, trust, compassion, and a sense of mutuality and respect form the essential cornerstones of all good relationships. Those with good relationships have the ability to communicate their disappointments to one another without attacking—and can enjoy each other's successes without excessive jealousy or envy. They can give, receive, and lean on each other without feeling dependent or weak. They can draw upon each other's talents and strengths and leverage them. We need to pass that message on, as well as the fact that certain defining events dissolve enmities that have lingered over a long period.

Mark, a once-strapping athlete, became severely ill. The immediate family gathered in support, but Mark's youngest brother went one step further. Although there had been a long history of bitterness between the two brothers, at this point the brothers put those feelings on hold. The younger brother tracked down Mark's long-retired high school football coach in the wilds of Maine to tell him of Mark's illness.

The phone rang one Sunday night. It was the coach. No momentous words passed between the two. The coach just wanted to remind Mark that he'd been one hell of a tough football player and could beat his illness with the same determination he'd brought to the gridiron a quarter-century before.

Mark cried himself to sleep that night, with tears of happiness and gratitude, that a brother with whom he'd had a tangled and complicated history would take the trouble to link with the coach; that the coach would take the trouble to deliver a message of caring, concern, and optimism. And he cried because a circle seemed to have been completed— old hurts erased, or at least softened, and a wellspring of good feeling opened.

―ଓ ଓ―

Many linkages are beyond comprehension. But as the Romans said, *"De gustibus non disputandum est"*—"There's no arguing about taste."

Corinne Lévesque described her relationship with her late husband, the charismatic former premier of Quebec, René Lévesque this way:

"What two people experience over twenty years—the highs and the lows, the joys and the sufferings, the strengths and the weaknesses, the big and small betrayals ... in short, all that constitutes the unique and complex chemistry between them, cannot be understood by others than them and them alone."

And there are all sorts of complementary linkages. There are Savers and Spenders who thrive with each other. There are Chartists, who map every contingency, and knee-jerk Gut Reactors, who link and flourish with each other.

There are Accelerators, who move and make things happen, and Brakers, who like to stop and watch the scenery, and they manage to get along because their own jagged edges find a peculiar match. The same remains the case with Birds that explore and Beavers that build nests—and Futurists, who try to predict trends, and those tied up in the past and for whom fourteenth-century illuminated manuscripts remain the perfect object for study.

I once consulted with two business partners, who were very different on the surface. One did all his analysis on a computer large enough to organize the Kennedy Space Center. The other, a technophobe, wandered around with his world on an index card in his shirt pocket. Yet they worked well because they shared a trust, filled in each other's spaces, and had a mutuality of purpose that cut through appearances and practices. Our differences allow us to link—in the same way that two asymetrical puzzle pieces find a way to groove together—but our similarities bring us together, too. Sometimes they're just not apparent on the surface.

⌒⌒

A bright MBA wanted to join a hot investment banking firm. He did all his homework flawlessly before going to see the partners.

The group loved him, and the managing partner told him so. "Jim," he said, "you impressed my people. You have a great track record. You clearly are hungry, and you want to do well. I have only one question left. Do you mind cleaning up crap?"

"What on earth do you mean?" the MBA said, startled. The managing partner, decked out in his power suit, shirt, and tie, recounted how he'd arrived on the red-eye from Los Angeles at six in the morning and taken a taxi right to the office to shower and shave and begin a new day. He'd gone into his private bathroom, flushed the toilet, and watched the system erupt before his eyes. Crap all over the place. It was too early to call the maintenance crew, so he had two choices: clean it up himself or leave it and wait for somebody else to make it disappear. He cleaned up the mess himself.

"Do you mind cleaning up crap?" he asked again. "That's the kind of partner I'm looking for—someone to share the downside as well as the upside, someone to accept responsibility, who can manage disappoint-

123

ment and failure as well as success, someone who can accept ownership for his problems. We're a high risk, high reward business. Can you manage all sides of the slippery slope? If you're not in it, we can't win it."

A link formed. A connection arose—based on trust and a sense of shared mutuality. Meaningful linkages are cut from that kind of cloth. You have to strive to be a mensch (applicable to both men and women)—to be decent and caring. To do the right thing—to do something over and beyond the expected. To be there when necessary and to not invoke convenient excuses or judge in a punitive way. Above all, to vibrate with a sense of humanity. And say what you mean and do what you say.

There are also many linkages that don't connect.

The reasons for this are legion. Sometimes two people decide to link, yet start with an insufficient amount of glue. Sometimes they harbor unrealistic expectations. Then other variables spring into the equation: misread promises, poor timing, limited communication, too many stresses, and an inability to get the other person to express his or her individuality.

Some don't understand that for a relationship to thrive there has to be a commitment to reciprocity. Some judge their mates excessively and view them through a psycho-microscope, analyzing every thought and action and not giving them a chance to breathe. And there are the counters who audit all the actions of others, making sure they're always ahead. They call to mind Matthew

10:30: "The very hairs of your head are numbered"—
and I know all of them. Nobody ever beats a counter.

A married couple went for a walk on a beautiful
spring night. Their marriage was on the rocks, yet the
wife was hoping for one last spark to keep things
alive. She suggested the walk, hoping that maybe the
beauty of the night would evoke feelings they'd once
had for each other,

They didn't speak until the woman looked up and
said, "Look at the sky! What a beautiful moon!"

Her husband responded, flat and cold, "Don't talk
about the moon. That's my moon."

She knew at that exact moment their marriage was
over. They flew to Mexico the next day to get a quick
divorce. They returned that night—and they slept
together for the first time in two years. Their love-
making was "deep, passionate, and reckless," as she
later explained it.

They needed to link and unlink and then link and
unlink again to overcome the toxic impact of too
many years of prolonged criticism, withdrawal,
deceit, and defensiveness. Perhaps their divorce freed
them from the commitment, obligation, and dependency they felt as a couple. They could unite as two
separate and independent parties without the fear of
being consumed by each other. Part of their paradoxical message was: "I need to trust you. But I can't.
Because then I'll need you." They haven't seen each
other since that last night. Theirs is a legacy of linking
by unlinking. Or, as another woman put it to me, "I
had to let him get in, so I could get out."

~◌◌~

We often think of sex as the ultimate linkage, and it may be. Exciting sex is both cephalic and phallic. The mind remains as important as the mechanics. Meaningful sex over a reasonable period of time involves communication and reciprocal creativity. It encompasses respect, surrender and vulnerability, mystery, passion, experimentation, and sensitivity. The great Persian epic poet Ferdowsi described two lovers being "as warp and weft." It's hard to imagine getting much closer than that.

The philosopher Ba'al Shem Tov put it succinctly: "From every human being there rises a light that reaches straight to heaven. And when two souls that are destined to be together find each other, their streams of light flow together, and a single, brighter light goes forth from their united being." That is orgasm in its total meaning.

A remarkable play on two Hebrew words reflects the essence of a valued relationship.

The Hebrew words for Man and Woman each contain three letters: [א י ש] and [אשה]. Take the two letters that are common to Man and Woman and put them together [אש] and they spell the word *Fire*. Take the two letters that Man and Woman do not share in common and put them together—and you come up with the word *God* [י ה] .

God signifies caring, respect and love, commitment, awe, and wonder. Remove qualities associated with God from a relationship and you get Fire, which for many of us represents anger, mistrust, disrespect, and deceit.

Yet join them all together as warp and weft, and you get Man and Woman and God and Fire, which is compassion and passion, caring and sharing, giving and taking, gentle warmth, and the consuming fires of mutual ecstasy.

Yet sometimes sexual linking can be a connection devoid of any closeness at all.

I consulted with a young woman who was referred to me as being "promiscuous"—a term rarely used in reference to men, whose similar actions would be referred to merely as "sowing their oats."

When I asked the woman why she slept with any person, she strongly corrected me. "I don't sleep with any person," she said, "I sleep with any *body*." Hers was a connection that completely dehumanized the intimacy of the sexual experience—yet it was the best she could do.

We also link with objects, symbols, and beings that aren't human—further proof of our very human need to ground ourselves, to feel connected. We Are All Citizens of the World of Stuff, reads a sign outside a Benedictine Abbey in the Southwest.

A woman called me one morning as I was about to leave for work. "He died. He died," she wept. It turned out catastrophe had struck overnight: Her entire house had burned to the ground; every bit of clothing and furniture she owned had gone up in smoke; every book and every keepsake she'd collected for over thirty years had gone the same way. An irreplaceable art collection had turned to ashes. Yet leading the list of casualties, in her mind, was her dog, who had died in the fire. Her most important link was gone.

This was a special "person" in her life. She had raised him. They celebrated holidays together. And together with her husband, the dog made up her immediate family. And now he was gone.

We should not dismiss these linkages, for many reasons. There are fifty-five million dogs in the United States—about one for every five people in the country. As the gifted writer Caroline Knapp put it in her book *Pack of Two,* we link with dogs because they give us something to touch and love. They never judge us when we falter or fail, they have no ulterior motives, and they are incapable of second guessing, complicated negotiations, and guilt trips. Dogs accept us for what we are and always have been—somewhat imperfect but always looking for a friend who will accept us on lenient terms.

Me? I still have the black and brown shoe brushes that I first used in the summer of 1957. I was working as a porter on the Canadian Pacific Railroad on the run between Winnipeg, Manitoba and Nelson, British Columbia, an old gypsum mining town.

Part of my job was prowling through the rocking corridors, collecting the shoes laid out for me, shining them bright, and returning them to the proper compartments before the first light of dawn.

I still have those brushes, more than forty years later. They say "Winnipeg" on them, the city of my mother's youth. They have followed me to five cities.

And I still love shining my shoes to a clear gloss.

I've promised to give the brushes to my children. Hopefully, they will give them to their kids. Four generations, receiving and giving, symbolized in a pair of brushes.

—ᏋᎧ ᎧᏋ—

Einstein said he believed that God did not play dice when he created the world, that things have a purpose and a meaning. William Blake put it another way:

The bird a nest.
A spider a web.
Man Friendship.

Our connections are infinite. We are who we are because we stand on the shoulders of those who preceded us, as those who follow us will stand on ours.

Each time I see linkages between events that were once mysteries to me, I learn something new. I feel the urge to share—to give those insights away—creating a new link.

Ecclesiastes said, "For one that is joined to all living things, there is hope," and I believe that's true. That is why we remain at heart progressive optimists rather than regressive pessimists. The more we connect, the less we need to look for beginnings and ends and causes and effects. The more we see the world as a circle rather than as a two-dimensional line, the more we are excited by the ordinary. The more we understand through our connections, the more we forge new trails and increase our understanding of the world around us—all the more reason to pass that understanding on to our children.

Native American poet Oriah Mountain Dreamer wrote one of the most eloquent invitations to link with another human being, borrowing imagery from both nature and James Joyce. I like her way of looking at the world.

It doesn't interest me where or what or with whom you have studied.

I want to know what sustains you from the inside when all else falls away.

I want to know if you can be alone with yourself and if you truly like the company you keep in the empty moments.

It doesn't matter who you know or how you came to be here.

I want to know if you will stand in the center of the fire with me and not shrink back.

I want to know if you can live with failure, yours and mine, and still stand on the edge of the lake and shout to the silver of the full moon, *"Yes."*

7

LIVING

Remember, people are unreasonable, illogical and
    self-centered.
Love them anyway.
If you do good, people will accuse you of selfish
    ulterior motives.
Do good anyway.
If you're successful, you'll win false friends and
    make true enemies.
Try to succeed anyway.
Honesty and frankness will get you nowhere,
    they make you vulnerable.
Be honest and frank anyway.
People favor underdogs, but they follow the top
    dogs.
Fight for some underdogs anyway.
What you spend years building may be destroyed
    overnight. I've seen that happen.
Build anyway.
People really need help, but they attack you if
    you try to help them.
Try anyway.
Give the world the best you have and you'll get
    kicked in the mouth.
Give the world the best you have anyway.

                    —*Anonymous*

WHEN A CROCK BECOMES
A PRECIOUS URN

A man I knew, David, lived his life to the fullest, sharing himself with others. He ran a successful business and was deeply devoted to his family. He was a leader in the community and gave to many charities. And when he became ill and was forced to take to his bed as he prepared to die, he saw life—all of life—pass before him in one afternoon.

As David lay dying in his bedroom, a funeral was planned. A circumcision was planned for his new grandson. A wedding was planned for his son. The out-of-town guests were arriving. The caterer came. The flowers were ordered. The phones were ringing. All as he lay dying.

It was strange, yet strangely beautiful. The endings and the beginnings, the joy and the sorrow, were all happening at the same time, and David witnessed all of it. As he lay dying, he did so in the full knowledge that life really does go on.

⟨∽⟩

In his novel *Northwest Passage*, Kenneth Rogers wrote, "On every side of us are men who hunt perpetually for their Northwest Passage, too often sacrificing health, strength, and life itself in the search, and who should say they are not happier in their vain but hopeful quest than wiser, duller folks who sit at home, venturing nothing and, with sour laughs, deriding the seekers for their fabled thoroughfare."

Living is a search for our own Northwest Passage. We experience bad luck but continue to search. We run up against obstacles but try to navigate around them. We meet opposition but push on regardless. Yet the marvelous part about living is that most of us keep going, not borne back ceaselessly into the past, but ever forward. In hope. Like David, we know that even if one life ends, living itself goes on.

Living is played out over time and centers around change, the taking of risks, the cycles of loss and gain, and the fostering of hopes and dreams.

We need to tell our inheritors that there is no such thing as a life without problems. Living is dealing with the unpredictable, the uncertain, the unexplainable, the unwanted, and the unfair. As the writer Kathleen Norris put it, with tongue firmly in cheek, "Life is easier to bear than you think. All that is necessary is to accept the impossible, do without the indispensable, and bear the intolerable."

None of us live in a friction-free world, void of stresses and scrapes. And just when we think we have order in our lives and things appear to be under control, a tremor may occur. "Life is fired at us point blank," the Spanish philosopher José Ortega y Gasset wrote. "We cannot say 'Hold it! I'm not quite ready. Wait 'til I have things sorted out.'"

As a result, we absorb this knock here and that knock there and are shaped by them. We make mistakes and find solutions. As Al Pacino remarked in *The Scent of a Woman*, the wonderful thing about dancing the tango is that when you mess up, you just "tango on."

***

I prefer to think of life as the Science of Uncertainty influenced by the Art of Probability.

For me, life is a science because we observe, conduct experiments, and offer theoretical explanations for why what happens to us really does happen to us.

It is a science with uncertainty and limited predictability, mystery, randomness, and contradictions. "It's a mistake to think it's the small things we control and not the large," Ann Michaels wrote. "It's the other way around. We can't stop the small accident, the tiny detail, that conspires into fate . . . But we can assert the largest order, the large human values daily, the only order large enough to see."

It is a science in that it follows natural laws, like the one that says the only constant is change and that the road not taken—or taken—makes all the difference.

It is a science, too, in that it constantly involves ever-expanding choices, even in something as mundane as having a cup of tea. I remember not long ago stopping for gas and a cup of coffee at a mom-and-pop store in a small town of 5,500 people in rural

Vermont. As I walked inside the station in the middle of nowhere, I discovered I had a choice of three kinds of coffee and five kinds of Chinese tea! Talk about choice!

Yet there's a paradox involved in all these choices. "People want to enlarge their choices, but by keeping all their options open, they actually diminish them," pollster Daniel Yankelovich put it nearly twenty years ago.

Life is an art, too, governed by smell, instinct, touch, and feel. We put our personal signature on the canvas of everything we do. We shape and mold our experiences and define our values. We give dimension to our actions. Discretion, instinct, risk, wisdom, and judgment remain the artist's skills in us, and we hone them through years of experience, uncertainty, regrets, successes, disappointments, and mistakes.

And probability plays a role, too. We have to figure the odds, not the guarantees. No matter how hard we attempt to control our lives, there are always limits to what we can accomplish. Man plans, God decides.

Those who work hardest will not necessarily be the most successful. Those with the most amount of "toys" will not necessarily end up the most fulfilled. Those who diet will not necessarily live better or longer. Assessing the probability involves tradeoffs. Those who smoke have less chance of getting Alzheimer's because they don't live long enough, while those who wear seatbelts and live longer see a greater probability of having the dementia of Alzheimer's visit them.

Yet it is the combination of science and art that makes us unique and defines our lives as one-of-a-kind. Add that elusive epoxy called imagination and we have a Sistine Chapel, a *Ulysses*, a Watson and Crick deciphering the elegant architecture of DNA, a Ted Williams batting .406, or a Tiger Woods mastering Augusta National in his first major tournament. Life is a kaleidoscope. Turn it one way and the image is brilliant and clear. Turn it another way and things fall out of focus. Every event and every moment is unique.

Life is a constant reminder of the cycles of time. We are endlessly in motion and constantly transformed.

The words of an anonymous poet express this all too well:

Look to this day for it is life,
For yesterday is already a dream
And tomorrow is only a vision.
But today, well lived, makes every yesterday
A dream of happiness, and every tomorrow
A vision of hope.

Our inheritors need to know what our distillation processes have taught us about the science and art of living—and I say this agreeing full well with Oscar Wilde, who said that "only the shallow know themselves."

The way we live depends on how we understand and perceive the world. Winslow Homer studied the Atlantic Ocean off Prout's Point, Maine, and mastered the artistry of waves as perhaps no other painter before or since. Perhaps he saw the ocean and its composite waves as the fluidity of life—never static, always moving, equilibrium always altered by the circumstances of the moment or the moon or rocks on the shore. That, in the end, is what living comes down to—waves and different forces all comprising a large ocean.

Take the word *Life* itself and break it down: the comings and goings; the stops and starts; the losses and gains, the hopes and despairs . . .

There's Life with the emphasis on one letter— LIFE. "I" people are masters of the universe in their own minds, at the center of everything. They feel entitled, exploit people, and have little or no empathy toward others. Every encounter is a win/lose game, and they need to emerge the winner, or their self-esteem, already low, will sink. They are more concerned with appearance than with substance. They have trouble forming long-term relationships. They feel easily wounded and alienated. As one woman put it, about her partner, with whom she'd just split: "We had a lot in common. We loved the same person. Him." What these people want most of all—to be valued and counted as special—eludes them because they lack the genuine commitment and sincerity to share and be concerned with others. They don't understand that what you want most in life you need to give away. And that's always been the case.

Then there's Life with an emphasis on two letters—LIFE.

"IF" people spend their lives thinking about what could or should have been, like Terry Molloy complaining to his brother, Charlie, in *On the Waterfront* that he "coulda' bin a contendah, instead of a bum, which is what I am. Face it."

"IF" people are preoccupied with their mistakes and regret the road not taken. If only I had a better wife; or had gone to a better school; or had a better job; or bought the stock that doubled. They're frozen in the past, unable to move on. The "retrospectoscope" is their instrument of choice. For them hindsight is a perfect science, but a sad one.

And too many "ifs" distort their sense of reality— as if their feet were planted firmly in the clouds.

Nadine Stair poked marvelous fun at this type of worldview when she was asked to write an essay, "If I Had My Life To Live Over." At the age of eighty-five, she identified herself as "one of those people who lives sensibly and sanely hour after hour, day after day ... who never goes anywhere without a thermometer, a hot water bottle, a raincoat, and a parachute."

Yet, marvelously and with a wry sense of humor, she said that if she had her life to live over again she'd concentrate more on eating ice cream and less on eating beans. "I would take fewer things seriously," she wrote. "I would climb more mountains and swim more rivers. I would start barefoot earlier in the spring and stay that way later in the fall. I would go to more dances. I would pick more daisies." And she vowed that at age eighty-five she would start. If not now, when?

Then there's Life with an emphasis on three letters—LIFE.

Mark Twain said that you should never waste a lie—because you never know when you're going to need one. We all lie to certain degrees, but there are those whose lives are built around the lie.

These people—described by Edith Wharton in *The Gilded Age* as "falsehood done in flesh and blood"—lack authenticity in anything they do, say, or believe. They lie to themselves and to others and thereby preclude any sense of trust or realness in their relationships. Some lie to exploit others. Others lie to cover up a dent in their psychic armor. And many who lie frequently lack the courage or maturity to be direct.

Then there is LIFE with an emphasis on all four letters. A full life acknowledges "I," and the importance of self-worth. The full life acknowledges that without "ifs" there would be no brainstorming, and that without mixing it up there would be no progress. Emily Dickinson acknowledged that lies are a part of life, but must be calibrated to the circumstances:

Tell all the Truth but let it slant
Success in circuit lies . . .
The truth must dazzle gradually
Or every man be blind.

Living is also movement, and with movement comes change. As G.K. Chesterton expressed it, "Progress is the mother of problems."

There is age change and work change and parents and kids change, success change, and failure change, too. And if you don't take change by the hand, it will surely take you by the neck.

We have changed our concept of the norm and raised the bar regarding our expectations. We are influenced by—but not chained to—the past.

As a result, we see ninety-year-olds taking up golf, eighty-year-olds romancing each other, seventy-year-olds running the Boston marathon, and twenty-five-year-olds running major corporations.

There are people with advanced degrees looking for part-time work, while a college dropout is the richest man on the face of the earth. There are women, CEOs of their homes, who transfer their talents to corporations and give the good old boys a much needed jolt. There are kids who get hell at home for smoking pot on a Thursday and on Friday learn that their father took delivery of a FedEx package full of cocaine at his office. Fifty-year-old fathers discover parenthood for the first time the second time around, and fifty-year-old mothers compete in the dating game with their seventeen-year-old daughters. Many parents are now not only parents to their children but parents to their parents as well.

There are teenagers dealing with the three R's— who suddenly realize they have to deal with a fourth R, Responsibility, as they encounter the complex choices associated with contraception, AIDS, drugs, abortion, and sexual preferences.

There have also been changes in how we relate to others, but not without its costs. A man I know spent sexually engrossed hours on the Internet in a cyber affair with a woman. When he suggested they meet, she said no, he would be disappointed. He persisted, and they met. His face immediately sent a message of disappointment. "I told you so," she said painfully as he left; they never connected again. Mystery was more powerful than reality.

There are changes that have an impact on self, family, and work, all rolled into one.

An entrepreneur came to see me. He was terribly disappointed with his life. He remembered his mother, a full-time stay-at-home woman whom he called a "permanent winter fire, sharing her warmth under all conditions." At the same time, he greatly loved his wife, a "liberated" woman who was involved in business ventures of her own.

He characterized himself as "an intermediate husband and father caught between yesterday and today with half-truths, half-beliefs, and half-realities. Searching for the right combination. I wish I could rid myself of guilt. "What I need," he said, "is my old-fashioned mother and my modern wife. So do my kids."

He had many contradictory ideas and images occurring simultaneously, all jumbled up, leading to unending tension between modern beliefs and old values.

What can we learn from this whirlwind of change? We have matured as a nation. We no longer indiscriminately accept what's placed before us as "good" because it feels warm and fuzzy, like the past. We should not mourn the past— especially one built with the help of stereotypes and founded on illusions. It will only impair our abilities to deal with our present and build our future. Perhaps Peter Drucker said it best when discussing managing in turbulent times: to deal with change we must be able to deal with the fundamentals carefully, consistently, conscientiously, and all the time.

And we need to pass that message on, received from the past and given to the future.

—☙❧—

A life well lived is a life of risk. Risk is not synonymous with uncertainty. It is understanding the laws of opportunity and probability.

Amos Tversky and his colleagues on the West Coast developed an interesting model of how most of us operate within four guidelines when it comes to taking chances. They're things our ancestors probably understood when they first got up the courage to venture into the cave.

First, they found, we prefer a certain outcome to a gamble. This is the impulse that leads many people to invest in bonds with guaranteed rates of return rather than stocks, which tend to have a roller-coaster lifecycle.

Second, we prefer to minimize risk rather than

chance a gain. This construct takes to heart the well-honed cliché that a bird in hand is better than two in the bush. Why chance the possibility of losing something you've already got, for something that might not be as good as what you have?

Third, we will assume a risk to avoid a loss. This scenario is what leads people to take toxic drugs to fight diseases. The side effects loom as less important than the certainty of the disease killing you.

And finally, we tend to compartmentalize when we take risks. We create silos in our thinking process and fail to connect things. We invest our money in long-term certificates of deposit, looking for the safe return, without linking the investment to the impact of inflation. Paradoxically, our gain could turn into a loss—if the rate of inflation rises higher than the fixed rate on the CD.

And many see risk in a light that is out of proportion to the actual circumstances. We should not allow ourselves to be like Sancho Panza in *Don Quixote*. At one point he spends an entire night desperately clinging to a windowsill—only to discover with the first light of dawn that his feet were only inches from the ground all that time.

But taking risks gives us hope to live for the future. As I saw written above the entrance to the Holocaust Memorial in Tel Aviv: "Remember the past. Live the Present. Trust the Future." That is the essence of hope, given the history of those horrifying events.

Little League baseball is a wonderful metaphor for learning how to take risks.

Go to a game on any spring evening and you'll often see the smallest kid on the team come to the plate and stand there with the bat glued to his shoulder.

He stands anxiously at home plate, his entire self-esteem tied up with how well he does. Not getting on base, with his teammates, parents, and grandparents looking on, would be tantamount to disaster.

But this kid is praying for a walk. You can just see it. His idea is to get on base without taking any risks or committing himself to anything. You can almost hear what's going through his mind.

If he doesn't swing, he doesn't miss the ball. If he doesn't swing, he won't strike out on three straight pitches. If he doesn't swing, he won't pop up to the pitcher or hit into a force-out or a double play. If he doesn't take any risks, in other words, he won't embarrass himself—except when he's called out on strikes. Then he can conveniently throw the bat down in disgust, kick his sneakers in the dust, yell a lot, and blame the umpire for his own failing.

But with good coaching and experience, certain things become apparent to him, and he sees risk in a new light. He realizes opposing pitchers have gotten his number when they toss three straight "meatballs" to the catcher and he goes down on strikes. He realizes he'll never get a hit unless he swings.

Even if the consequence of swinging is a weak "nubber" to the first baseman, he comes to understand that good things happen when you take risks. He learns that lesson after his first hit bullets through the middle between the pitcher's right ear and the shortstop's gloved left hand.

And he further learns that the best hitter in baseball failed to get a hit at least two times out of every three at bat. Pretty soon he'll be sizing up the catcher's arm strength and weighing whether it's a good risk to try to steal second.

The legacy we need to leave is that we have to learn to judge the risks and take them. For taking no risk is the greatest risk of all. The writer Peter Bernstein points out,

> The revolutionary idea that defines the boundary between modern times and the past is the mastery of risk—the notion that the future is more than the whim of the Gods and that men and women are not passive before nature. Until men and women discovered a way across the boundaries, the future was a mirror of the past or the murky domain of oracles and soothsayers who held a monopoly over knowledge and anticipated events.

You can't put life on hold—because when you stop risking you stop living in many ways.

A man who consulted me complained that his life lacked excitement and purpose and could be summed up in three numbers: thirty-seven, twenty-eight, and forty.

"I'm thirty-seven years old. I have twenty-eight more years to go. I make forty thousand dollars per year, and I'm unhappy." I asked him how come he was so sure he had twenty-eight more years to go. He told me to do the simple math: "Thirty-seven plus twenty-eight equals sixty-five, and that's when I plan to retire."

Frankly, his attitude jeopardized his chances of holding on to the job for another twenty-eight years.

He saw the "no risk" course of staying put and tending his hearth fire as being the safest alternative to leaving and looking for something else to do. He discounted twenty-eight more years, waiting for sixty-five, assuming he would get there. He banked on the safety of not taking a chance, never realizing that choosing not to take a chance was tantamount to choosing not to live.

———— ❧❧ ————

Part of living is acknowledging a sense of scale, but also acknowledging that the scale, in human terms, is miraculous all by itself and wonderful to behold.

I never fully understood the true meaning of the world *miracle* until a depressed, disconnected woman of nineteen came to see me. I'd always thought of miracles in terms of Moses parting the Red Sea or Jesus raising Lazarus from the dead. It wasn't until Nancy came to see me that I understood the root of the word, in Latin. "*Mirabile dictu!*" the Romans used to say ("Wonderful to speak of!") or "*Mirabile spectu!*" ("Wonderful to behold!") A miracle is something that is wonderful to behold.

Nancy had attempted suicide, partially because, she said, life had no pulse and was too boring. "I'm just normal in everything I do."

After five minutes of deep thought, I said, "Normal is a miracle."

We sat looking at each other in silence. "To move a finger up and down is a miracle," I explained, wiggling my forefinger. "Try to understand the neurophysiology. You can't build a robot that extends and flexes its digits on command. It's remarkable."

To a color-blind person, seeing shades of color is a miracle; to a victim of severe glaucoma, reading is a miracle; to a mother of a handicapped child or someone deprived of freedom, normal is a miracle.

"We need not wait for a church to canonize us before we become the fully conscious beings we were meant to be," the writer Richard Bode wrote recently. "If we fail, we pay for it with our lives. I mean that literally, for the consequences of indifference to the little wonders of the world are all too plain."

And we need to tell our children that you reach a certain point in a full life where you appreciate the concept of "bonus time." It's a time when you genuinely savor the good things in life and see them as bonuses rather than further acquisitions. These can be anything from taking in Monet's water lilies at Giverny to biting into an ear of freshly picked corn on the cob before tasting the sea bass you caught that morning as the sun was coming up. The splendor of simple things.

Living is also the acknowledgment and embrace of hope, the last creature to escape Pandora's box.

Hope is the solvent that cuts through the impossible and offers the promise of a better future. It's the glue that integrates our being and the magnet that attracts our resources and acts as the antidote to fear. "To hope," wrote Erich Fromm, "means to be ready at every moment for that which is not yet born, yet not to become desperate if there is no birth in our lifetime."

One Sunday I received an emergency call at my house. An eighty-year-old woman had become suddenly depressed two weeks before, and her family was terribly worried. Prior to that she swam every day, had lots of social connections, and was well in tune with life. All of that had stopped.

I met them at my office and was introduced to an elegant woman of great dignity and beauty. She was pure Boston Brahman, an aged version of a portrait by John Singer Sargent. And she was clearly in pain.

As we talked I noticed that her body movements and speech came very slowly. It was as if she was operating underwater. When I asked what was troubling her, she said she didn't know.

"Has anything unusual happened to you lately?" I asked.

"No," she replied.

"Is your husband alive?"

"No."

"When did he die?"

"Five years ago."

"Have you been ill?"

"No."

"Have any of your friends been sick?"

"No."

Each time I asked her something, she responded with the minimum number of words and made no attempt to expand or explain. After twenty minutes of questioning, I had absolutely no understanding of what was causing her problem. I switched the direction of my questions.

"Are you dating anyone?" I asked. She seemed puzzled by the question. Hesitantly, she replied, "What . . . do . . . you . . . mean?" Her back straightened and her eyebrows arched ever so slightly. A light suddenly appeared in her eyes.

"I mean, do you see men on dates?" After a brief moment, she replied, "Yes."

"Are you dating anyone in particular," I asked.

"Yes."

"Do you like him?"

"Yes."

"Do you see him frequently?"

"Yes."

"Are you sleeping with him?" I asked.

"That's a very personal question," she spat. "You're impertinent. Like all psychiatrists, you're interested in nothing but sex, and you're awfully young to be asking that question." I agreed I was young and impertinent but asked the question again. "Are you sleeping with him?"

"Yes," she replied defiantly, almost shouting. "But he dropped me two weeks ago!"

She lowered her head and described the pain, shock, and hurt she had been feeling for the past two weeks. She opened up like a day lily in June.

It was her loss of hope—her fear that there was something wrong with her—that depressed her to the point of feeling she'd never be able to find another relationship again. She looked at her future and saw nothing but loneliness and emptiness.

We talked for a while more, and she left, after agreeing to come see me at my office in a couple of days.

On the appointed day, she arrived transformed. She was alert, bright-eyed, and vivacious. She looked years younger than her true number, and a strong vitality had returned to that Sargent face of hers.

"What happened to cause this turnaround?" I asked, smiling broadly.

"When I left your office," she said, "I thought you were the rudest person I had ever met. I vowed never to return here again. But when I got home and was about to put the key in the door, thinking about your persistent, rude question, I felt an enormous surge of relief.

"And then I said: My God. He doesn't see me as an old crock but as a precious urn. He sees my strong sensual needs as those of a vital, attractive woman with the same sexual desires as younger people. And as I thought about that, I was filled with hope. And I said to myself, 'That young man is my friend.'" What

I had shared with her was the gift of hope. Yet in a strange way she had given me hope, too. We can't go on living without it, that I know. Another legacy, and that I know, too.

◦⌒◦⌒◦

I'm impressed by those I've met who should have given up hope but didn't: those with great personal losses; those held back by profound physical limitations; those abandoned by irresponsible parents.

But one thing I've noticed about people who never abandoned hope was that they believed in themselves and didn't buy into the negativity around them. They are able to extract positive things from dismal events and see the bright side. They will let go of their pain and move on. They accept that they are their own primary agents of change and build alliances. Like the seasoned sailor, they know they cannot control the wind . . . but they can control the sails. They have tasted success in the past—and their palates have strong memories.

And they know that to risk is to adapt—and that therein lies the hope to live. "For to try and fail is at least to learn, but to fail to try is to suffer the loss of what life might have been."

8

LEADING

The heights by great men reached and kept
Were not attained by single flight.
But they while their companies slept
Were toiling upward through the night.

—*Henry Wadsworth Longfellow*

Schmoozing and
Microschmoozing

My first semester in medical school was one of the most difficult times in my life. I found myself overwhelmed by the work, and, as a result, I pushed too hard and pulled all-nighters to keep up with the neverending stream of information. But the harder I studied and pushed, the less I absorbed and remembered.

After I flunked my first anatomy exam, my gears came to a grinding stop, and I knew I was in trouble. So I went to see my psychiatry professor, looking for some kind and magical words.

"You need to stop feeling sorry for yourself," Dr. Michael said bluntly, after listening to my troubles. "Get off your ass. And go back to working the way you always have. And have some fun."

I was taken aback, floored. I'd gone to see him expecting some brilliant remarks couched in technical jargon. Instead, he gave me advice head-on—and it worked.

Dr. Michael read me well, and his insight put the responsibility for my failure right where it belonged—

back on my shoulders. I lightened up, put myself on a realistic study schedule, and I never looked back academically after that. I learned that he who splits his own wood warms himself twice.

We later became colleagues—and good friends. What had started as a mentor/mentee relationship emerged into a closeness that allowed us to spark off each other. Dr. Michael was a remarkable leader. He had a passion for his work and was generous to a fault. He had great vision. His willingness to risk and question old norms and theories proved an inspiration. He prized and rewarded independent thinking above all else. Studying with him on a regular basis, I felt galvanized, motivated, and moved.

But Dr. Michael was also a personal disaster: He was a chronic gambler who played the ponies and lost heavily; he was terrible with managing money, childlike in his needs, chronically late for everything, plagued by ghosts that kept him awake at night, and totally insensitive to his own health. He was, in other words, not the model leader most of us would actively seek out.

But I connected with his excitement and wisdom, his ability to cut through complex issues, his empathy, and most of all his "realness." Those qualities, not his shortcomings, made him a wonderful leader to me.

Our relationship taught me several important things: Mostly it taught me to throw away all the innocence I'd harbored about leaders. Leaders are real people, not idealized, omnipotent beings. They come with talents—and with flaws, very much like our

Navajo blankets. And I learned that all leaders are partial leaders—even the best never cover every base all the time.

—⁓⁓—

Late in his life, Picasso said, "When I was a child, my mother said to me, 'If you become a soldier, you'll be a general; if you become a monk, you will end up as the Pope.' Instead I became a painter and wound up as Picasso."

Picasso's words get to the core of leadership. Strip away all the things we associate with great leaders—charisma, charm, courage—and you come down to three essential and intertwined qualities that involve the head, the heart, and the feet: an idea that connects them to people (head), an ability to inspire them (heart), and a mastery at moving them in a particular direction (feet). They are the antithesis of Edmund Burke's admonition that all that is necessary for the forces of evil to win in the world is for good enough men to do nothing.

But as Picasso also hinted, leaders have a belief in their own talents, a vision, an independent way of thinking, physical and psychological endurance, the courage to risk and blaze new trails, and a passion for a cause.

There is no crisis of leadership in this country, as many would have us believe. Rather, there is a crisis in the way we think of leadership. There are plenty of leaders—just no messiahs to galvanize all of the followers all of the time.

One day as I was walking through the halls of a Boston law firm I saw a note from an eight-year-old, the child of one of the firm's partners, pinned to a bulletin board. The memo was all questions:

"How do I become famous? How do you become a writer? Who do I ask? Why do people always want more? Why does medicine taste so bad? . . . Why are some people so enthusiastic and others so bored? Did God mean us to be civilized? Was I meant to be this way? People are always on such a stronghold with their ideas—Why?. . . What makes people mean or nice?"

The boy was a mind-leader—and his father had the wisdom to recognize that quality in his son, which is why he chose to post the memo in public—to keep people on their toes.

The boy connected with me. He inspired me to think. Why, as we get older, I asked, do we gradually cease ending sentences with question marks and end them more and more with periods? Real leaders never really age in that sense. They have a perpetual restlessness—the inquisitive innocence of the child combined with the seasoned wisdom of the experienced adult. They ask questions and look for ways to reframe solutions. That everlasting question mark is as important a legacy as any we'll ever leave.

Leaders stretch. As legendary ad man David Ogilvey put it, "Leaders grasp nettles"—they grab onto prickly issues and deal with them, influencing us to follow their lead—because there is something innately inspiring about watching someone negotiate a handful of thorns and emerge victorious. They're in effect saying: "There. I can do it. Now, so can you."

—⌀⌀—

Most people who lead are neither heroic nor celebrated. They are at home raising families, teaching moral and ethical principles. They are in schools, transforming minds. They are in synagogues and churches, elevating consciousness. They are in hospital emergency rooms, saving lives.

They coach football, edit newspapers, and serve on the boards of charitable organizations. They run businesses that provide opportunities for thousands. "Many who have shaped history are buried in unmarked graves," Eric Hoffer wrote. "It is a mark of a creative milieu that lesser people can become instruments for things greater than themselves."

Even so, leadership remains a vital issue in corporate America. It makes the difference between a mediocre company and one that amounts to something that's truly outstanding. Yet the role of a single leader spreading his or her magic dust through a company is overrated.

Entire institutes and departments at universities dedicate themselves to studying and teaching leadership. But a leadership seminar does not make a leader—any more than studying a sailing manual makes a competitive ocean racer. You have to think and plan and make it happen all the time and live in the trenches (or in the sail locker with the swabbies.)

True leaders earn their stripes. They decode complex issues and communicate their solutions simply. They know intuitively that a solution inevitably creates a new set of problems. They convey a sense of trust and confidence in their troops and don't hesitate to delegate. They know what they're up against—and don't offer weak excuses when things turn momentarily sour.

A leader is not a leader just by virtue of title, position or force. True leaders, rather, seem to know that leadership revolves around an understanding of four interlocking elements: a knowledge of the personal side, developing relationships between people, the context in which they work, and the role of timing.

David Halberstam captured much of this in his delightful book *The Amateurs* on the sport of rowing. "A good crew meant shoehorning some eighteen hundred pounds of meat and ambition and ego into a thin shell that weighed 180 pounds and then making it work," he wrote. He went on to describe the role of the crew's true leader, the Stroke, who sets the pace and timing. "Shealy believed that all people sought symmetry and purpose in their lives, something that lifted them up and made them feel better about themselves. And here were eight oarsmen having worked so hard and sacrificed so much, catching something magical and doing it race after race, each oarsman making the others better."

━━⚘━━

And real leaders are there when the maelstrom appears.

After two serious downturns in the market, the CEO of a mutual fund company sensed a great unease in his colleagues and sent out a long and thoughtful memo to everyone in his shop.

He cut through the complex issues and set a pragmatic course for the future. He admitted his own limitations, and his note was laced with humor, honesty and a realistic perspective. "Don't look for a market prediction in what follows," he wrote. "I'm not smart enough to forecast, or dumb enough. If I was and did, you wouldn't believe me anyway. And you'd be right. . . . If you're feeling anxious, you have plenty of company. Hard-won performance has disappeared overnight. Of course it hurts."

He went on to say that the firm had written to its clients and asked them to exercise calm and caution, perspective and realism.

Everything he said was backed up by facts, yet what came through most in the memo was a sense of personal identification with the concerns of his colleagues. And he ended with a sense of challenge, not defeat—and a charming and kind sense that he trusted their individual judgment, expecting them to deal with both continuity and change. A problem, he suggested in as many words, can become an opportunity not yet discovered.

"We should follow our own advice," he wrote. "Ours is a business of relative performance. We have to play the cards the market deals us. If we can remember that, come to work every day to do the best we can under the circumstances handed us, we will work through this period of volatility, as we have worked and succeeded through every other.

"We have grown so quickly, and become so much better, that many people here have not experienced the kind of setback we are going through. It happened before. Most of our shareholders and clients proved loyal. The company continued to earn profits. Bonuses continued to be paid. If we are sensible and focused, we might gain competitively in this environment."

The company rebounded very nicely after a time, and I attribute its ability to weather the storm to the CEO's innate understanding that screamers and those who panic don't lead people well. Bullies can lead for an afternoon but can't lead for even a full week without major fallout. This CEO got his company through the storm because the crew could see the captain on deck doing the same things they were. He also gave them a sense of empowerment, which by its very nature involves leeway and the chance to make mistakes and learn from them. He seemed to understand that

To be successful
One needs to make good decisions.
To make good decisions
One needs to get experience.
And to get experience
One needs to make bad decisions.

Good leaders have extraordinary antennae that connect with their people.

Not long ago I worked with a dynamic man who had an uncanny ability to sense the needs of his staff.

One Friday morning as we were walking down the hallway we passed a young woman. Wayne asked her why she looked so down in the dumps. She told him that she was exhausted yet still had a ton of work to do before the day was done.

"Sheila," he said, "If you could do anything you wanted right now, what would it be?"

"Probably, I'd go home and sleep for a couple of hours," she replied, "and then get a baby-sitter and go see a movie with my husband."

"Do it," Wayne responded. And with a twinkle in his eye and a Cheshire Cat smile, he said, "And while you're at it, you and your husband have dinner on me. If I see you around this place at any time this afternoon, I'll fire you." The following week I ran into Sheila again. "Now you can understand why he owns me," she said to me, almost blushing.

Some people have a circuit breaker that doesn't allow them to connect, particularly in certain environments.

Steve was one of the smartest people I ever knew. He had impeccable academic credentials and had worked for a number of successful companies. He appeared to have all the necessary qualities for running a company. But as became apparent, he knew nothing about context when it came to leadership.

He was hired as the president of a company

founded by two entrepreneurs. They had the good judgment to understand that the growing company needed someone versed in "systems," not their seat-of-the-pants management style. Steve was their natural first choice.

He kept the founders abreast of everything that was going on at the company. But his sense of urgency and feel for the people differed dramatically from theirs.

The culture they'd fostered was feet-on-the-desk blue-skying, a lot of schmoozing, brown-bag lunches, and throwing ideas around for the hell of it, often late into the night. The founders had been oxymoronic leaders, managing to be both casual and intense, funny and serious, loosey-goosey and focused. That was the culture of the company they needed Steve to manage.

Steve's modus operandi was three-hour formal meetings, written agendas, heaps of computer print-outs, and using the word *task* as a verb.

One culture sang improvisational jazz; the other formal opera, and the twain would never meet.

The founders recognized this and went to Steve to share their concern. Appealing to his technical background, they asked him to "microschmooze" a little more. He understood the concept of microschmoozing in an intellectual way, so he readily agreed to follow up on the founders' suggestion. But it was a forced effort at best.

One day I passed Steve's office and stuck my head in the door. He explained his dilemma about the clash of rhythms but figured he'd found a solution. Proudly he showed me his calendar. He'd blocked out an eleven-thirty to noon slot once a week for microschmoozing. He had totally missed the spirit of the concept. Spontaneity seemed beyond his understanding and practice.

I knew he wouldn't make it. And he didn't. He just couldn't connect with the culture he'd been brought in to lead—demonstrating that you can graduate Phi Beta Kappa and still flunk running a company.

Yet I also worked with a leader who lacked elegance but who mastered a work environment.

John was a bull in a china shop. He took a sleepy, risk-averse service company and turned it into a dynamic organization. And he was a melting pot of contrasts: demanding and understanding; insensitive and perceptive; combative and contrite; short-tempered, loud, and condescending but also gentle and supportive. Lots of people were intimidated by him and went out of their way to avoid him.

Yet many also admired him for the way he redefined the ordinary and did not buy into stereotypes, and for his accessibility, commitment, and dedication. He never bore a grudge. He knew how to deliver bad news—always with a suggestion on how to make things better. He was a leader who told you hard things to your face and said nice things behind your back. His people came to understand the culture he was trying to build: to turn a sleeping giant into a nimble colossus, they needed to be flexible and fast, argumentative, creative, and driving, to maximize shareholder returns so they could survive and thrive in the next millennium.

⁓ ⁓

Timing is as important in leadership as it is onstage. Some leaders do best when a rising tide lifts all boats. Others blossom during crisis. Their pulse quickens; they take charge, set goals, delegate, hold people accountable and find excitement from creating order out of chaos. That's when they earn their chevrons. And some have the unique ability to sense the moment, or as the Greeks call it, *Kairos*, seizing the now and running with it.

Still others find themselves able to jump start a pulseless organization, as Robert Kennedy did when he inherited a lifeless Justice Department in the early 1960s. He understood that "the first task of concerned people is not to condemn or castigate or deplore; it is to seek out the reason for disillusionment and alienation."

Yet some so-called leaders engender feelings of antileadership, disillusionment, and alienation through their lack of understanding of the importance of timing.

In the summer of 1986, I sat in a small conference room in the huge and opulent corporate headquarters of a major home furnishing company outside Chicago.

I was there to help a group of mid-level managers come up with a "coping strategy." The company was being taken over; hundreds of workers were shell-shocked. It was unclear who was to stay and who was to go. The managers were scared but tried to look composed. Yet it was clear that despite our mission in the room—figuring out how to spread a cohesive message throughout the corporation—everyone was concerned primarily with Number One.

The managers began to talk among themselves.

The leaders of the company were going to walk away with fortunes the size of which none of the middle managers could even begin to comprehend. Yet it was their job to smooth the way and clean up the mess—to deliver the jolting news of the takeover and explain its ramifications to the ordinary Joes around the rest of the company.

"It makes no sense," said one thoughtful manager. "At the same time we're letting people go, others in the company are getting rich." And what was the rationale? asked another manager. Increasing shareholder value? Did the privileged few ever risk their own equity? Why should they be the only ones to reap rewards? asked another manager, clearly dealing with his own frustration. Weren't the top guys well paid to start with? And isn't deploying resources and bolstering those in distress part of their jobs? asked still another. What about the troops left holding the fort and those let go? Shouldn't they share? How long can this thoughtless behavior continue before it affects productivity? asked one. This was 1986. The wave that would become a tsunami had yet to make its true shape apparent around the world. The same questions echoed through conference rooms all around America, Europe, and the Pacific Rim in the years that followed.

Insensitive decisions take on the cloak of immorality. Leaders of many companies forget that the flipside of inspiration is distrust, alienation, and indifference, and that the flip side of connection is fragmentation.

This kind of fragmentation spawns a cover-your-ass attitude in the survivors: Never go out on a limb, cover mistakes, never volunteer—and always give the appearance of being busy. The net effect remains that the operation will never be as good as it could have been, and that those forced out will carry the baggage of mistrust and cynicism on to the next job. Is that a legacy we want to leave?

＊＊＊

When our first child left to go away to college, I gave her a small slip of paper, the size of a business card, to keep in her wallet. It read:

- Set goals
- Work hard
- Have fun
- And never act out of panic.

I made sure to include the last piece of advice because I've seen a number of leaders panic under pressure and explode the entire system they were working to build.

They lose perspective and fail to understand relationships. They fail to prioritize and delegate. They play to the crowd, trying to become all things to all people and end up losing the confidence of their constituency.

A good leader knows how to calibrate power and influence. There's a story from the Crusades, in which King Richard I of England goes to meet with Saladin the Turk to demand the surrender of Jerusalem. With typical Plantagenet zeal, Richard draws his giant two-handed slashing sword and brings it crashing down on a helmet sitting on the table between them. The helmet, not surprisingly, is cleft in two. Saladin observes this act and responds. He draws his curved scimitar, places it sharp-side up on the table and drops a delicate silk scarf toward it. The scarf meets the blade and two silk scarves flutter to the floor.

We need to tell our inheritors that at certain times leadership requires howitzers and at other times it simply requires elegant restraint.

By nature, leaders tend to be restless. They stretch, and when they enter new arenas, they learn, often painfully.

Jim is a wonderful fellow who conveys the confidence of a natural leader. He went to a first class university, rowed on a Henley crew, and started a successful business on his own. But when he decided to run for public office in his town, he ran up against a brick wall.

He was hanged in the local press, vilified under an avalanche of criticism. All in public, to boot. And he was devastated. It hurt. He was used to controlling situations, emerging victorious, and being rewarded. He'd never run up against anything like this before—and his three kids were reading all this stuff about him in the papers. The combination just about flattened him.

But he recouped. He grew to understand that leadership involves taking knocks as well as strong positions, and he came to appreciate the words of architect Walter Gropius, that "it takes strong conviction and faith to carry the ball when the onlookers are hooting."

Those who find themselves able to rise above disappointment and continue on with the essence of life inspire us, and because they inspire us, they lead us. Through the very act of leading, they remind us that we as humans have forged what is essentially a progressive society—one that is always on the move, moving "forward," even when the true direction seems up for debate.

─ ⁀ ─

Leaders also have a sense of humor that embraces the dilemmas of life—because they've lived them.

"Several writers have compared old age to a shipwreck," wrote one leader, then age eighty. "You jettison one thing after the other, throwing various gear overboard to stay afloat. I still have my port and starboard lights—they are a bit dimmer, but they work. My compass is OK, but my gyroscope needs adjusting. The rudder still works if I run slowly, but the boiler room is in a hell of a fix. One runs on Social Security and prunes."

I prefer leaders who readjust their compasses rather than capitulate as they enter difficult periods in their lives. Ben Franklin invented bifocals at the age of seventy-four. Georgia O'Keeffe painted well into her nineties. We all have our own leaders who connect and inspire us. I'm reminded of a college president who was blind and deaf, a young man with an addiction who hit rock bottom and then rebounded, and a woman with three small kids who lost her husband yet took charge and carved out a meaningful life. I know a competitive squash player with a prosthesis below his knee, and a gardener in his eighties who takes precious care of my copper beach tree.

We all have the capacity to lead, because in our own small ways we have done something to inspire, something to grab the imagination of another and set it free.

Emerson was not referring to leaders in particular when he wrote these words, but they capture as well as any the heart of the issue of leadership for us to pass on:

> To win the respect of intelligent people and the
> affection of children.
> To earn the appreciation of honest critics and
> endure the betrayal of false friends.
> To find the best in others.
> To leave the world a bit better,
> Whether by a healthy child, a garden patch or a
> redeemed social condition.
> To know even one life has breathed easier
> because you lived.
> This is to have succeeded.

9

LEAVING

No one is beat 'til he quits
No one is through 'til he stops
No matter how hard failure hits
No matter how often he drops.
A man's not dead 'til he lies
In the dust and refuses to rise.
Fate can slam him, and bang him around
And batter his frame 'til he's sore.
But no one can say that he's downed,
While he bobs up serenely for more.
A man's not dead 'til he dies
Nor beat 'til no longer he tries.

—Edgar A. Guest,
"Heap of Living"

"But It's My Leg"

Boys and girls from all over the world come to Boston's hospitals for treatment of complicated disorders and are helped by sensitive, dedicated, and talented people.

Eric, a nine-year-old boy, entered the hospital suffering from bone cancer in his right leg. A group of consultants agreed the best treatment would be to amputate his leg below the knee.

Eric's parents were advised of the decision, and they consented. The orthopedic surgeon went to visit Eric and told him what needed to be done.

"I don't want to lose my leg and be crippled," he cried. "Can't you do something else and let me keep my leg? Can't you just cut out the tumor?"

"I wish I could but I can't," said the surgeon. "This is the best treatment for you. We're going to give you a new leg, not as good as the old one, but you'll still be able to do lots of things that you did before." But Eric held his position. No surgery. The doctor left and returned several hours later.

"I know you're frightened," the surgeon said. "I would be too. But it's the best way we can cure you. I was thinking you'd be like Ted Kennedy's son. He had a similar problem, lost his leg, and look what he can do. He skis." Eric reluctantly agreed to the procedure.

After the operation, the surgeon came to see Eric to say that everything had gone well and that in a short time he'd get a new prosthetic leg.

"But I want my old leg back, too." Eric said. "Where is it?" The surgeon was shocked. The tumor was on its way to becoming a teaching slide, and the rest of the limb had been thrown away.

"I told you," the surgeon said. "We removed it." "I know," Eric said. "But I want it back. *I said you could take it off, but I never said you could keep it! Why can't I have it back? It's my leg.*"

It never occurred to the surgeon—or anyone else—to return the leg after it had been removed. But after all, it was Eric's leg. He felt entitled to own it, to look at it on his own time and mourn the fact that it was no longer attached to his body.

To leave means to say good-bye, to let go, and move on. It invariably means a sense of loss.

We cannot leave and not grieve, even when our losses are welcome. Saying good-bye to a thorny problem or a failed marriage or a bad job engenders a sense of loss. People who give up smoking or drinking because they have to, in order to keep living, grieve terribly—because they may be leaving behind the best friend they ever had in the world. Never mind that the friend or lover was going to kill them one day.

Loss is around us every day. We see it in those who suffer from illness or who have been held back by profound physical limitations. We see it in children abandoned by irresponsible parents. We see it in those who have been knocked down, courageously get up with a renewed spirit, only to be knocked down again.

Yet cycles of loss and gain remain intertwined. We're born every time we breathe and create, and we die many times in life, too—when we lose a loved one, or something special to us.

Life is a cycle of loss and gain, and our bodies deal with this every moment. Red blood cells live six to eight days and are replaced with new ones. The cells die, regenerate, and die again—so that in a very real sense birth means an end to death and death means the beginning of new life. Acts of creation and destruction occur simultaneously, even as the end of winter means the beginning of spring, losing one season only to gain another.

To believe one can actually avoid loss in life is to think one can be exposed in a rain storm and not get wet. It's just not possible.

Yet we humans have shown a remarkable ability to deal with loss when it does occur. Our resilience in the face of repeated losses and adversity mark us as the ultimate survivors. Somehow, even when we all lived in the forest, we learned that wounds eventually heal, that the one-eyed man could still see, and that the heart grows strong when it encounters many setbacks. God, it's been said, put us on our backs so we could look up.

Even those with multiple losses often score later on. Ugly ducklings at age fifteen turn into beauties at nineteen. Kids hooked on drugs, written off by their peers and parents, rebound and become outstanding citizens. Those who repeatedly fail in business sometimes hit the jackpot later on, and many with serious illnesses say "Hell, no," recover, and make medical statistics lie.

We need to delete the word *loser* from our vocabulary because a loss at one point can turn into a gain later on. *Citizen Kane, The Maltese Falcon, The Philadelphia Story, The Wizard of Oz,* and *Bonnie and Clyde* all came up "losers" in Oscar competition. Yet they all became film classics.

We alone have this sense that life often imitates a series of waves; that loss can be turned into gain; and that leaving and loss are just punctuation points in life. As Richard Nixon (no stranger to loss himself) wrote to Ted Kennedy after the Chapaquidick incident in 1969: "A man's not finished when he's defeated; he's finished when he quits."

This understanding that we rebound and get on with life marks us for immortality. It is our "Amazing Grace"—a quality we need to let our inheritors know we received from our past.

How we manage loss depends on the sum of a whole series of events—some canceling each other out, other making things worse. What the loss means to us depends on how we have dealt with loss in the past, the power of the blow, what else is going on in our lives at the time, the supporting or nonsupporting characters around us, and our ethical, moral, and spiritual perspective on life.

The differing degrees of intensity, pervasiveness, and frequency weave into each other like strands of cotton in a shirt. They dictate the shape of the garment we wear.

And further complicating matters is the universal rule that there is no universal rule for gauging what specific losses mean to different people. We need to tell our followers all of that.

⸻ ❧❧ ⸻

Two stories—one sad and one funny—illustrate dealing with loss. Both involve me.

I was beset with a palpable sense of loss when our youngest left for college. The house was too quiet. I missed hating my son's loud music and endless phone calls. I missed worrying about him if he came home too late. I missed the arguments. I missed everything about mixing it up with him. His new independence was clearly a gain for him, but a loss for me.

One warm fall evening, I pulled my car into the driveway, and I sighed at the sight of a lonely basketball lying at the verge. I noticed the desolate hoop and realized that I hadn't heard that knotty "swish" sound or that clanging, metallic "ka-boink" rebound noise in weeks. There was nobody to play Horse with. The last of the Horse players had left home in August.

I got out of the car and set my briefcase and jacket down on the driveway as I walked over to retrieve the basketball. I dribbled once, twice, the bounces seem-

179

ing to echo hollowly off the walls of the house.

I pivoted, turning my back to the basket, still dribbling, moved to my left, and arched up a difficult hook shot toward the basket. The ball soared off my fingertips, and the next thing I heard was that beautiful sound of the swish as the ball fell through the netting.

I looked up, smiling, proud of my shot, wanting to cheer—and be cheered. But there was no one around. The last of the cheering section had left home in August. And I felt very lonely.

Now certainly the loss itself was not sudden or unexpected. We'd known he'd eventually move out after eighteen years! I should have been well prepared: our two other kids had left home before, and I'd dealt with those losses well.

But I knew that the episode meant that I was getting on in years—and that it was time to be born again in other ways. And I dealt with it by seeing the loss not as an ending but as another beginning—while looking forward to playing Horse again at Thanksgiving time.

A few summers ago, my wife and I went to visit the Baseball Hall of Fame in Cooperstown, New York—probably so I could bathe in the reflected glory of the Brooklyn Dodgers of my youth.

I visited a pitching range several blocks from the hall itself. It's a neat setup where you throw at a tarpaulin with a bull's-eye on it, and a special Tru-Pitch radar machine records the speed of the pitches. The machine gives you a digital readout on a "gen-you-ine" certificate. I had three tries at a target twenty feet away. An absolute piece of cake.

I almost dislocated my right shoulder on the first pitch, but managed to unload the next two with a certain amount of brio.

I raced over to the Tru-Pitch to get my certificate, figuring I'd probably registered somewhere in the 60- to 70-mph range. My heart sank as I watched certificate #106569 scroll out of the machine. There had to have been some kind of mistake. The readout said my top-speed pitch was a paltry forty-three miles an hour.

People may laugh, but I was shocked. The precipitant event had been sudden—and I was disturbed in part because I had set myself up for loss absent a true appreciation of my ability. I suspect we're all legends in our own minds when it comes to using our imaginations in the context of boyhood heroes, and I had simply assumed I could throw as hard as Sandy Koufax or "Rapid Robert" Feller, especially at that short a distance. Twenty feet. Sheesh.

But my sense of loss did not continue for long. The image of a great pitcher jumped immediately into my head.

Nolan Ryan struck out over five thousand batters by throwing the ball sixty feet, six inches, at 90 mph every fourth or fifth day for over two decades. And here I'd almost broken a wing notching a mere 43 mph over a distance of twenty feet.

In retrospect, I needed to experience the disappointment to truly appreciate his achievements: not just knowing academically, but knowing in my gut, too.

Mine was a minor loss but an important one.

When the loss is major and gets handled in a brilliant way, the results become all the more impressive.

⌒☙⌒

Two out of every three Americans will lose their jobs at some time during their lives because of company cutbacks, plant closings, or mergers—or because they have principled disagreements with colleagues or bosses and just decide to cut their losses and walk. And they'll lose their jobs because sometimes they just lose "it." As Arthur Miller described Willie Loman in *Death of a Salesman*, a play that still moves me to my very bones: "He don't put a bolt on a nut. He don't tell you the law or give you medicine. He's a man way out there in the blue, riding on a smile and a shoeshine. And when they start not smiling back—that's an earthquake."

And for many, losing a job is just that—an earthquake that has more than economic consequences. For many, losing a job can knock down all the surrounding supports—like a bowling ball hitting the kingpin at a perfect angle and knocking over the other nine pins for a strike.

When my friend Arthur lost his job, he was just one more victim of the wave of reengineerings that swept America in the eighties and nineties.

The layoff came as sudden and shocking. Yet Arthur's sense of perspective and ability to keep his loss from becoming a long-term disaster proved nothing short of masterful.

The following note arrived in my mailbox, postmarked June 9, a couple of years ago:

Arthur Fisk invites friends and foes to suggest some place to which he might report for work at 9 A.M. on Wednesday, August 1. Until that time, both groups may reply to 1128 Fullerton Ave., 02138.

Now, did the notice land Arthur a job? I don't think so. But what it *did* do was call out a cast of supporting characters to help him cope with his sense of loss, fear, and isolation. The note acted like a radio distress signal on the high seas—the equivalent of, "I've just been struck by an iceberg, and the ship is taking on water fast. Please sail to coordinates ... Mayday. Mayday." (We may forget that Mayday, the international distress signal, comes from the French *M'aidez*—"Help me.")

Arthur's sense of loss diminished as a result of his Mayday signal. People called him, commiserated, and invited him over for dinner—not out of pity or fear that he would starve but because Arthur almost goaded them into it. "This isn't contagious, you know," he'd quip over the phone, angling for a dinner invite. "In fact tomorrow's *New England Journal of Medicine* has an article that proves you can't get 'job loss' through casual contact."

Arthur seemed to understand the words of poet Naomi Shihab Nye. "Walk around feeling like a leaf," she wrote, "Knowing you could tumble any second/Then decide what to do with your time."

Peter, the director of a scientific research center at a major technology company, found himself in a terrible position. He had just learned that he would have to close the entire center and lay everybody off—including himself.

The event was sudden, and though not completely unexpected, the massive scale of the shutdown certainly was.

There was no way for Peter to measure everyone's reaction to the closing. He was dealing with the differing personalities of literally hundreds of people. No one can measure such a situation without conducting an exhaustive study—not something one does before announcing a plant closing.

But Peter knew that the loss had a terrible potential to metastasize. He understood what they call the "multiplier effect" that could lead to a cascading series of catastrophes for his employees: a blow to self-worth, feelings of isolation and embarrassment, a negative impact on family life, and increased vulnerability to physical and psychological problems.

He took the only responsible course he felt he could take. He played the leadership card.

"I thought you might like to hear this from me," Peter wrote in a long and thoughtful memo. "My job now changes from being an advocate for the center to being your personal advocate . . . The closing in no way reflects on you. I know no finer group of people to work with. How privileged I feel to have been here." The words might sound formulaic or out-and-out corporate phoney to some. But I know the man.

So did his employees. They knew he meant every word he said.

The note was eloquent, full of caring for the psyches of his employees. He made it clear that this was the future and that it was best that they all put this sorry event behind them, cut their losses, and move on. And then he closed:

> Finally, I welcome the opportunity to meet with you one-on-one. As you know, I am an early bird breakfast eater. If lunch and a stroll in the neighborhood makes sense, book me in. Keep the glass half full. Keep the socks rolled up. Keep the spirit and dignity intact. Keep the wind at your back. And when you need help, you'll get it.

What a moving statement of caring! His authenticity, sympathy, eloquence, and expression of solidarity helped keep the sense of loss among his people from spreading like fire on cellophane. In two pages he did more to help the health of his employees than probably all the HMOs in the city: He saw that to hope is to cope; and that to cope is also to hope.

―◦◦―

Perspective works both ways—and it's important that our inheritors understand that one person's catastrophic loss can pale in comparison to another's far more real loss.

While working on the manuscript for this book, I

realized one holiday afternoon that I'd lost some critical notes. I spent the better part of the afternoon and most of the evening ransacking my study and house in search of them, but no notes surfaced.

I went to bed, frustrated and angry—and woke up at four-thirty in the morning with this clear-as-a-bell sense that the notes might be in my office in Cambridge. So in the predawn darkness I set off for Harvard Square.

After an exhaustive search of my office, I soon realized that my record stood at zero for two, home and away, and sat down at my desk completely demoralized. With nothing else to do—and no light yet in the sky—I decided I might as well start sifting through the mail that had been left at my door over the weekend.

The junk went into the wastebasket. The envelopes with postage stamps and human handwriting went into a short pile of their own.

I opened a letter from a man I'd consulted with on business matters several years earlier. Quickly I realized he was asking to consult me on an entirely different matter.

His son, Roger, a valedictorian and Ph.D. candidate at a midwestern university, had been diagnosed as a schizophrenic. He was homeless and living in public restrooms in Chicago. The father had managed to get Roger to admit himself to a hospital on several occasions, but he had left on his own and stopped taking his medication. The father didn't know where his son was and was trying to track him down.

Could he come by and see me to talk the next time he was up in the Cambridge area?

My office windows face west, so that I could see the sunrise only as it reflected from the windows across the way from me that morning. I know that was fitting, now. My loss was just a pale reflection of this man's. My loss was retrievable. His was not.

Losses also differ by the degree.

When Harry was laid off from his job, he and his wife decided to hide his furlough from their children lest the news upset them, so they lived a facade of normalcy.

But the kids began to notice some subtle changes. Their father appeared less meticulous in his dress. He left for work later in the morning and arrived home earlier than usual. He got more calls at home. He lost weight, and he became edgy about spending money.

After a few months, the kids approached their parents, terribly concerned—convinced their father had cancer and was trying to cover it up.

Harry and his wife decided to spill the beans, realizing their charade had taken on a dangerous life of its own. The kids' reaction? "Is *that* all?" they cried in unison. "Gee, Dad, come on. You'll get another job!" And shortly thereafter, Harry did.

Dealing with loss also entails a certain amount of courage and maturity. I know a young woman who keeps the Jewish high holy days because she finds genuine renewal when she atones on Yom Kippur.

Just starting out in a new and important job, Hedy was asked to organize a major business trip to the West Coast. The opportunity was a real coup for her because she was the new kid on the block, and the offer to organize the trip meant that someone thought she had the potential to become a rising star at the firm. The trip would mean three solid days of meetings from morning to night, and she was thrilled to take up the challenge.

Her sense of anticipation lasted until she looked at the calendar and realized that the three-day trip encompassed Yom Kippur.

"We needed to do the project," she told me. "I was an essential member. I wanted to change the date, but the plans had been made. I was anxious about rocking the boat. And so I went. I lacked the courage to change things. I was disappointed with myself. I felt I had sold out, and that I had traded off years of tradition for a quick business fix." Hedy spent as much of that day reflecting and repenting as she would have in any synagogue. She reviewed her life and confronted herself as never before as to what was important and what was nonnegotiable. In the end, she felt she had grown up again by dealing with her loss, her conflict, and her gain. Prayer was her way of thinking. For her, it was both a ritual and a practice. And it didn't need a formal place to legitimize its expression. Sometimes you get a Hobson's choice, in which both doors reveal tigers and we have to choose the one less ferocious.

That's a legacy we must leave behind, too.

A child born at the time of the Roman Empire had a life expectancy of eighteen years. By 1900, life expectancy worldwide had risen to forty-nine. A person born today can expect to live to the age of seventy-five. By the year 2050, the number of people over the age of one hundred will be more than 800,000.

The flipside of a longer life, though, is the potential for loneliness and incapacitation—and the question of how to live those unaccustomed years.

And it's remarkable how a sympathetic ear can make an enormous difference.

Molly was an eighty-year-old widow who lived alone. She viewed one of the crowning achievements of her life as having provided for her six sons. Coming in a short second was her pride that the six boys had forged successful careers for themselves. Yet the fact that they chose to make their work in cities far away was a disappointment.

Her six boys came to visit her infrequently. When they did visit, they exhibited all the classic signs of wanting to leave right after they get there. She knew they loved her. It was just the residue, Molly knew, of leading fast and involved lives. Yet she said to me once, "It's strange how one mother can take care of six sons and six sons can't take care of one mother." What she wanted to know was whether she mattered to them in soul and spirit, captured in a line of St. Augustine—"Whisper in my heart. Tell me you are there."

At one hospital, doctors see Mollies in the emergency room every day—victims of indifference who come in distressed, feeling abandoned and that no one, anyone, cares about them anymore.

The doctors at this hospital have a special diagnosis when they see people like Molly: the NNFDK syndrome—*No Naches From Der Kinder*—"No Pleasure From The Kids." It's a sense of abiding loneliness compounded by a belief that while an investment—in the kids—has paid off, the same investment has failed to provide the long-term return they originally hoped for: comfort and companionship in the older years.

The NNFDK syndrome is rooted in an age-old belief that things would somehow remain the same forever, that life as we know it would never change. Yet Buddhism focuses on certain immutable truths and asks its followers to meditate on them daily:

I will grow old.
I will become ill.
I will die.
Everything I like and cherish will change and
    become separated from me.
These actions I own.

That kind of acceptance decreases our tendency to cling to our selves and our possessions. It's painfully true and at the same time difficult to practice—but increases our awareness of the responsibility we have for our own actions and puts our lives and those of others in perspective.

Beyond working toward acceptance, treating the NNFDK syndrome is not simple. Certainly it helps having a supporting cast really listen, express interest, and show respect. Most of these people respond positively, and their relief from pain may be one of the reasons medical placebos actually have healing powers. Placebo comes from the Latin "to please," and someone attempting to please a person by paying attention can ease the pain of loss.

Yet on the other hand Molly's dilemma sends an important message to all of us: We need to set aside inviolate time to pursue independent interests—and develop a sense of community outside the family and not be exclusively bound to even those close to us. We need to find activities that meet our needs separate from others, so that, when left alone, we can relish that sense of "unlonely aloneness" that will get us through the days when we feel lost and left behind. As William Blake put it:

> He who binds to himself a joy,
> Does the winged life destroy.
> But he who kisses the joy as it flies,
> Lives in eternity's sunrise.

And sometimes we hold on to things it would be in our best interest (it seems) to lose.

A saw a man with a remarkable sense of "body logic." He was immaculately tailored and shod. His curly dark hair bore the signs of elegant barbering, and the fragrance of aftershave lotion wafted around him as he entered my office. He weighed close to 350 pounds and stood but five feet, ten inches tall. The first thing he said was that he was there only because his wife was concerned about his health.

"I know I'm big but I never get out of breath," he said. "I'm light on my feet and look good in my clothes. I don't sweat and my blood pressure's pretty good. If my wife or anybody else sees me as fat, they don't understand that if I'm fat, it's the healthy kind." Unhealthy fat, he explained, came about as a result of putting all kinds of junk in your body. That was not the case with him: he ate prime meats, Godiva chocolates, fresh vegetables, and special pastries. He rode around in his Cadillac between appointments munching on salamis. But the salamis were fine, he said. They were kosher—so they had to be!

Similarly, I consulted with a woman crane-like in her appearance. She was very bright and animated, but I had trouble focusing on her words because her sleeveless baggy sweater and tan shorts could not disguise the fact that she was wasting away. She weighed eighty-six pounds, a drop of forty pounds over the past year. And, she said, she felt "full" all the time.

She had categorized foods into "friends" and "enemies." The friendly and safe ones included lettuce, carrots, diet Cokes, and a special whitefish. The enemy foods were pasta, bread, any kind of meat, and all edibles that had "fat" listed on the product label. If she could lose just a few more pounds in her thighs, abdomen and bottom, she said, things would be OK.

They each had their own body image that they zealously wanted to preserve. Any change—especially a forced one—would be seen as dangerous and followed by a profound sense of loss.

——————

Some losses are almost too great bear and are inexplicable.

Tony was a sensitive seven-year-old who came to my office with his concerned mother. He was a good student and very active in the Catholic church. His father was his special buddy, and the two of them spent a lot of time together practicing hockey drills. Then one afternoon Tony's father died suddenly in a freak accident.

Initially Tony showed no outward emotion in response to the loss of his father. He continued to go to church every Sunday—yet each time Tony set off for church, he would ask his mother when his father was coming back. She responded by saying as gently as possible that his father had died, that he was now in heaven, and that he would not return.

Six months after his father's death, Tony began to show overt signs of grieving. He was confused and angry, seemed preoccupied, had trouble getting to sleep, and bombarded his mother constantly with questions about why his father couldn't come back. He refused to attend church.

Tony sat in my office and said, "God's not fair."

I asked him why.

"I go to church every Sunday and pray for my father to come back. But he doesn't come. That's not fair. I love him and want to be with him. God's son died and He brought *Him* back. If He can do that, how come He can't bring my *father* back? Why is God so selfish?"

What do you say to Tony? Do you tell him that Jesus was more important than his father? Not to Tony. Do you tell him that God's act in bringing his son back was a miracle? To Tony, his father was a miracle. Do you tell him that God prioritizes and plays favorites? Does that mean that Tony or his father are not one of God's special people? Do you tell him to trust the system and that life will balance out? Do you say that life's not fair and give him plenty of examples? Do you tell him that he'll be the recipient of special things at a later point to compensate for his loss? No one can say that and have any credibility. Nothing can make up for the loss of his best friend, teacher, mentor, and father. Especially at the age of seven.

None of those replies would have sustained any meaning for Tony. His request and logic were simple: I love my father. He was special. I lost him. I miss him. I've played by the rules. Life should be a quid pro quo. Now, give him back to me.

I didn't have any answers that made sense for Tony. Or for me. I don't know why things like this happen. Any answer I gave him would be what T. S. Eliot described as "a hint followed by a guess," and I didn't want to trivialize his questions.

I needed to help Tony mourn, to be with him, to allow him to express his rage and to hope the healing process, with the help of others, would minimize his pain.

In time, I think, he will join all of us in trying to put in place an acceptance that many things just don't make sense and some events have no solid answers. And I can't give him a pat answer just to satisfy my own sense of inadequacy.

I don't like the word *retirement* because for many it has come to mean a permanent loss of work, a loss of engagement and activity. And to many it signifies a precursor to the ultimate loss—of life itself.

Carl worked long and hard and invested well. Through it all he never really liked his job. He just did it as a means to an end: making and saving enough money so he could do the work he wanted to do—no work.

Carl retired at sixty. At first he loved it because it meant no more sweaty, crowded subways, no more missed lunches, and no more anxieties about being evaluated by younger bosses.

Every day was an open day. Every night he could stay up and watch the late movie. He had no schedules and no demands.

It worked for a while. But soon each day seemed to pass imperceptibly into the next. He felt no contrast between feeling tired and feeling relaxed. He lost the sense of what it was like to look forward to a weekend. There was a sense of "eventlessness" in his life.

Carl began to slip. His focus and interest narrowed. He stopped reading the newspaper and began to find television boring, especially the news. Calling his friends or going to the movies became a major event. And he complained about everything from the cost of food to the "decline in moral values."

Soon he began to experience vague aches and pains and a buzzing in his ears. He spent endless hours visiting doctors. All the evaluations were negative. Doctors gave him a bunch of technicolor pills to "calm him down"—with no success. But he kept coming back, week after week.

Carl, you see, had found a new line of work—medical work. His preoccupation with his body, his attention to his unwelcome guests, and scheduling doctors visits became a full-time job for him. He had unretired.

Unfortunately, Carl's new job gave him no more pleasure than his previous one. He retired at sixty, died psychologically at sixty-five, and was buried at seventy. He had a plan for stopping work; he just had no plan for living in retirement. It's important to pass on to our children the wise saying that it's better to wear out than to rust out.

Henry Wriston, former president of Brown University, put it this way: "Retirement can be lonely, drab, frustrating—but so can a job. If you dull the mind, the world will be drab. If your mind grows, as it should, retirement is exciting."

⚬⚬

I prefer the term *retirements* because I feel the term reflects a truer picture of what happens in life. We retire many times.

We retire from the ranks of the single when we

marry. We retire from the ranks of the married when we divorce. We retire from the ranks of the led to the ranks of the leader when we take on more responsibility. We retire when we forsake singles for doubles in tennis and jogging for curling, golf, and long hikes in the woods. We retire at a later stage when we pass on ideas and concepts to protégés we trust to carry on our work.

All we're doing, in fact, is trading something old for something new. Retirements are not just the closing of a chapter but the opening of a new book. And that is a legacy I want to leave—that all closings are followed by openings and that every time we leave something behind we have the potential to pick up something new.

We can't love without running the risk of losing. We can't successfully learn without the fear of being dismissed. We can't be accomplished workers without the concern of not achieving. We can't really laugh unless we lament and deal with pain. We can't link meaningfully unless we give up some of our own needs. We can't fully live until we understand that there is "a time to live and a time to die." We can't lead dynamically unless we give up some of our power and share it with others. And we can't properly leave without opening a new chapter, in this case, a legacy. As an anonymous poet wrote:

After a while you learn the subtle difference
Between holding a hand and chaining a soul.
And you learn that love doesn't mean leaning

And company doesn't mean security.
And you begin to learn that kisses aren't contracts
And presents aren't promises.
And you begin to accept your defeats
With your head up and your eyes open
With the grace of a woman, not the grief of a
    child
And learn to build all your roads on today
Because tomorrow's ground is too uncertain for
    plans
And futures have a way of falling down in mid
    flight.
After a while you learn that even sunshine
Burns if you get too much.
So you plant your own garden
And decorate your own soul
Instead of waiting for someone to bring you
    flowers.
And you learn that you really can.
That you really are strong
And really do have worth
And you learn
With every good-bye you learn.

EPILOGUE

For me to have made one soul
The better for my birth;
To have added but one flower
To the garden of the earth;
To have struck one blow for truth
In the daily fight with lies;
To have done one deed of right
In the face of calumnies;
To have sown in the souls of men
One thought that will not die;
To have been a link in the chain of life
Shall be immortality.

—Edwin Hatch, *Immortality*

Uncle Walter's Ashes

Our journey is long or short. We don't know which. Most of us are not so wise (or is it arrogant?) as to assume we know the "measure of our days."

We traverse a territory between the blooming buds and the falling leaves that is both rough and smooth, through a life of risk and being involved with others.

We proceed and stumble, nurse our wounds, and move on, searching and learning, ready to try again in the hope that things will get better and that dangers will abate.

Our passage is filled with many surprises. Some we conquer and grow by; others overwhelm us. But we continue on our relentless course, encountering a host of ideas and people along the way. Our innate sense of caution helps us sort out those that are nurturing and loving from those that are evil, hostile, and dangerous. And some transform us in ways that we once thought unimaginable.

All the while we are building our legacy.

Through everything we do, and everything we

experience, we build this legacy. And as we traverse our one-of-a-kind journey—one we never truly complete—we pass on to others the meaning and specialness of our lives, which have never been lived before and will never be lived again.

⸻

I recently lectured a group of sixty bright young entrepreneurs who run their own businesses as part of a special university program, "The Birthing of Giants." For an overnight assignment I gave them a series of questions to think about for the next morning's discussion: What has life meant to me? What has been important in my life? Who has influenced me? What have I learned? What has excited me? Where have I stumbled? What have been my blue points? What mistakes did I make and how did I correct them? What has been my understanding of success and failure? What were my proudest moments, and what did they mean to me? What things have I left undone? What would I like to do?

The morning's discussion was like trying to move a barge without a pole. Vacant looks. Stares. Silence. I asked one young woman for a comment, and she kind of stammered for a moment before summing up the courage to speak. "I have two small kids," she said. "I'm in my thirties, and my business is just starting to turn a good profit. I'm on a roll. These questions depressed me. They all seem to deal with the end of life. I'm not ready for that."

I smiled and asked how many of the group did

financial audits at the end of the year. Sixty hands went up in unison. "Then tell me," I said, "why is a financial audit more important than a personal audit? Why should living life take second place to a group of numbers? This is *life* we're talking about here, not *death*." Eyes lit up. I could almost hear lightbulbs clicking and smell insulation burning. They understood—and enthusiastically got into the discussion.

That's what a legacy is—a personal audit that we construct around our own individual experiences in Loving, Learning, Laboring, Laughing and Lamenting, Linking, Living, Leading, and Leaving.

Our net worth is more than simply the calculation of our assets minus our liabilities. Our net worth includes how we lived our lives, the contributions we made, and what mattered most to us.

There will be many who are critical of our lives, but we can't really control that. Theodore Roosevelt put it well:

It is not the critic who counts. Not the man who points out how the strong man stumbled or where the doer of deeds could have done better. The credit belongs to the man who is actually in the arena, whose face is marred by dust and sweat and blood; who strives valiantly; who errs and comes short again and again because there is no effort without error and shortcoming; but he who knows the great enthusiasm, the great devotion; who spends himself in a worthy cause; who at the best

knows in the end the triumph of high achievement and who at the worst, if he fails, at least
failed while daring greatly, so that his place
shall never be with those cold and timid souls
who know neither victory nor defeat.

A comedian who wrote his own material showed
some jokes to his producer, who immediately began
to tear into them unmercifully. "This is terrible," the
producer said, running a red grease crayon across a
page. "This is awful." And he continued nonstop.

"Hey," the comedian responded. "Not so fast! All
you do is criticize. Where were you when the page
was blank?" We all start with a blank page. And no
one among us can really judge the quality of our
material until we've led complete lives. And that by
its very definition is an impossibility. No one ties up
all the loose ends.

Auguste Rodin worked on his *Gates of Hell*
sculpture for three-and-a-half decades. These magnif-
icent doors were a metaphor of man's spiritual and
physical yearnings, an epic of human passion and
folly. Yet this achievement, this work that preoccupied him for thirty-five years, stood unfinished when
he died and eventually had to be cast posthumously.

While life may be finite and incomplete, our legacies carry the potential to make our lives infinite and
purposeful. I think that's what Saint Francis had in
mind when he said, "It is by dying that one awakens
to eternal life." A more contemporary view came
from George Bernard Shaw, taking issue with

Macbeth. "Life is no brief candle for me," Shaw said. "It is a splendid torch which I have got ahold of for a moment, and I want to make it burn as brightly as possible before handing it on to future generations."

⸻ ❧❧ ⸻

The important part about handing that torch to future generations is capturing its essence before it goes out.

At the end of her long and full life, my mother came down with Alzheimer's disease. She stared emptily into space or at some meaningless television screen for hours on end. Her words, if she ever spoke, came out slurred and dull. Often I'd go to visit her and try to make contact. I'd sing her some of the old songs—an odd mix of Canadian prairie and Brooklyn—and she'd briefly come to life, a short glimmer of recognition registering and then fading. It was like watching a window shade go up and down again.

But after a time even the old songs failed to make much of an impact. I'd leave these visits feeling so sad that sometimes I'd get lost on the way home, a distance of only four miles.

One day I tried something different to register a spark. "Mom," I said softly. "I've just finished writing a book on job loss and its impact on the lives of individuals, families, and communities."

After a moment of silence, in an absolutely crystal-clear voice, my mother said, "Tell me. Is that a concern of yours?"

She had heard. She had understood. I cried and I hugged her. It was clear to her why I had written the book—as a way to work through the pain we had all gone through watching my father lose his job during my teenage years. A whole life as I'd known it came back to her in an instant.

I had fired a spark that lit the torch again, and I left the nursing home that day with profound feelings of both happiness and regret. I was happy that we had lit the torch. I was happy that she knew I carried with me well into my adult life the legacy of the hard years.

But my greatest regret was that I couldn't keep the torch lit long enough to distill its essence and get more stories of the old days to pass on. Even the greatest advances in medical science would not let that happen. The torch burned briefly and then went out. But heat and light remain to this day.

We create legacies all the time. Some people build skyscrapers. Some pass on stories. Some write them down. No culture is without its legacies.

A friend has on his study wall a photograph of Sri Lankan fishermen sitting in chairs on high stilts in the water. The overall effect of the photograph is that you're looking at a photo of a series of Giacometti sculptures lined up against a humid red sky.

The stilts and attached chairs are passed down from generation to generation like seats on the New York Stock Exchange, from father to son, mother to daughter, a basis for sustenance and life for generations yet to come.

A legacy, to be effective, has to capture our "realness" in that way. You can't draw a circle around a bullet hole to create the illusion you've just hit a bull's-eye. We owe it to our descendants to give them our opinions with the bark on—otherwise a legacy can become a list of meaningless platitudes and Polonius bromides.

The name Theodore Geisel does not register with many people, but he's very real.

The charm in a commencement address Geisel gave comes through his voice—or, more accurately, the voice for which he had become known—the voice of Dr. Seuss:

"My uncle ordered popovers from the restaurant's bill of fare. And when they were served he regarded them with a penetrating stare." I think every eye must have lit up at that moment, hearing the cadences that had carried them through *The Cat in the Hat* and *Green Eggs and Ham* in their youth.

"Then he spoke great words of wisdom, as he sat there on that chair: 'To eat these things,' said my uncle, 'You must exercise great care. You may swallow down what's solid—but you must spit out the air.'"

And then Geisel closed:

"As you partake in the world's bill of fare, that's darned good advice to follow. Do a lot of spitting out of the hot air. And be careful what you swallow."

Certain legacies are so real—and so powerful—that they produce an intuitive reaction in those who receive them. They just know what to do.

Uncle Walter was born in Brooklyn. He obviously suffered some genetic mutation because he became a rabid Yankees fan.

Before he died, he asked to be cremated. Yet he left no instructions on what was to be done with his ashes. The job fell to his favorite nephew, Peter.

Peter decided to go to Yankee Stadium one day with Walter's ashes in a plastic bag. It was "Socks Day" and every paying customer got a pair of midnight blue Yankee socks. Peter salted Walter's ashes into the socks, and when the appropriate time came, he joined thousands of other fans on the field before the game.

He waved his Walter-laden socks around and around over his head and Walter's ashes came out and wafted through the bright summer afternoon; they settled all over the grass, the infield, and maybe even on the bust of Babe Ruth in center field.

The Yankees won the World Series for the first time in nearly two decades that year, and I'm sure Walter's ashes had something to do with it. Legacies are magic in that way, even if you don't believe in magic all the time.

A colleague had been very ill. Yet he pulled through and decided one morning to drive out to the huge stone chapel at his old prep school to thank God for his deliverance.

He'd always appreciated the cleverness of the school's founder, he recalled, and the way he situated the chapel. As every boy left the building, his eyes were immediately drawn to the hills of New Hampshire in the distance.

The words of the 121st psalm were supposed to resonate, and they did:

> I lift up my eyes unto the hills. From whence
> comes my help? My help comes even from the
> Lord, who made heaven and earth . . . The
> Lord is your keeper; the Lord is your shade
> on your right hand . . . will keep you from evil
> . . . will keep your life . . . will keep your going
> out and your coming in from this time forth
> and for evermore.

My colleague stood at the door of the chapel, looked up at the hills, and repeated the psalm from memory, reciting a legacy left for him by a man he'd never known but who'd left it for him nonetheless, knowing it would be needed someday. And he believed more than ever the words of T. S. Eliot: "At the end of all our exploring, /Will be to arrive where we started and know the place for the first time."

<hr>

I began writing the prologue for this book at the time of Passover and Easter. It is a time when Jews and Christians share a common bond—memories of being incarcerated and then freed, of having a dynamic leader who presented moral, ethical, and spiritual templates that have served as guides for all our lives. It is a time of promises and responsibilities, and a time for hope for an eternal life passed down through generations.

The prayer we said that night at the conclusion of our Passover seder captures the spirit of both faiths. In itself it remains a marvelous legacy to pass on.

> May we never become too complacent not to
> notice ills in the world.
> May we never become too comfortable in our
> homes to forget the homeless.
> May we never take our freedom for granted,
> forgetting those who are not free.
> May we never accept anything our government
> does without checking to see whether it is a
> moral act.
> May we never forget to use our voices, our time,
> our energy to make this a better place to be.
> May we never lack the vision that things can and
> should be better.

We are the essential immutable links in the legacy chain. As the poet said, "The clock of life is wound but once"—we should not fear that life will pass too quickly and come to an end. Our concern should be that we have a beginning and a middle that we can celebrate. For it is not so much what we have left undone in our incomplete lives that matters as much as what we have contributed.

We need to remember the gift of the Roman god Janus, who bore the ability to look both into the past and into the future. We can share that vision and wisdom—and pass it on: receiving from the past, giving to the future.

While there are limits to adding years to our lives, there are no limits to adding life to our years. We can do that, appreciating and handing down treasures greater than material wealth, the gifts that we have received from our forebears: the treasures of what we have learned about Loving, Learning, Laboring, Laughing and Lamenting, Linking, Living, Leading, and Leaving.

As John Kennedy said in 1961: "When at some future date the high court sits in judgment on each one of us, our success or failure in whatever office we may hold will be measured by the answers to four questions."

Were we truly men and women of Courage?
Were we truly men and women of Integrity?
Were we truly men and women of Judgment?
Were we truly men and women of Dedication?

That is up to us.
We do make a difference.
Our lives have never been lived before, and will never be lived again. Capture that specialness—and pass it on.

Selected Bibliography

Abrahams, Israel. *Hebrew Ethical Wills.* Jewish Publication Society of America, 1948.

Becker, Ernest. *The Denial of Death.* The Free Press, 1973.

Bernard, Chester. *The Function of an Executive.*

Bernstein, Peter. *Against the Gods: The Remarkable Story of Risk.* John Wiley and Sons, 1996.

Bode, Richard. *First You Have to Row a Little Boat.* Warner Books, 1993.

Brenner, Harvey. *Mental Illness and the Economy.* Harvard University Press, 1993.

Bronowski, J. *The Common Sense of Science.* Harvard University Press, 1978.

The Ascent of Man, Little, Brown & Co., 1973.

Buchwald, Art. *Leaving Home.* Fawcett-Columbine, 1993.

Camus, Albert. *The Myth of Sisyphus.* Vintage Books, 1955.

Cousins, Norman. *Anatomy of an Illness.* Bantam Books, 1981.

de Botton, Alain. *How Proust Can Change Your Life.* Pantheon Books, 1997.

Drucker, Peter. *Managing in Times of Great Change.* Truman Talley Books/Dutton, 1995.

Dyson, Freeman. *Disturbing the Universe.* Harper & Row, 1979.

Erikson, Erik. *Childhood and Society.* W. W. Norton, 1950.

Feder, Leonard. *The Ten Challenges.* Harmony Books, 1997.

Fitzgerald, Faith T., M. D. "Decisions about Life Threatening Risks." *The New England Journal of Medicine,* Volume 331, No. 3, July 21, 1994.

Fromm, Erich. *Man for Himself.* Fawcett Books, 1947.

The Revolution of Hope. Bantam, 1968.

Gaardner, Jostein. *Sophie's World.* Berkley Books, 1996.

Gardner, M. Robert. *On Trying to Teach.* The Analytic Press, 1994.

Greiff, Barrie Sanford, and Preston Munter. *Tradeoffs.* New American Library, 1980.

Groopman, Jerome, M. D. *The Measure of our Days.* Viking Press, 1997.

Halberstam, David. *The Amateurs.* Fawcett-Colombine, 1985.

Heschel, Abraham. *Who Is Man?* Stanford University Press, 1965.

Hoffer, Eric. *Reflections on the Human Condition.* Perennial Library, 1963.

Kaufman, Stuart. *At Home in the Universe.* Oxford University Press, 1995.

Knapp, Caroline. *Pack of Two.* Dial Press, 1998.

Koop, Sheldon. *Even a Stone Can Be a Teacher.* Jeremy P. Archer, 1985.

Lightman, Alan. *Einstein's Dreams.* Warner Books, 1993.

Luria, A. R. *The Mind of a Mnemonist.* Harvard University Press, 1968.

Maugham, W. Somerset. *Summing Up.* Penguin Books, 1963.

Michaels, Ann. *Fugitive Pieces.* Alfred Knopf, 1996.

Moyers, Bill. *The Language of Life.* Doubleday, 1995.

Negroponte, Nicholas. *Being Digital.* Alfred Knopf, 1995.

Nye, Naomi Shihab. *Words under the Words.* The Eighth Mountain Press, 1995.

Osler, William. "Books and Men." *Boston Medical Surgical Journal,* 1901.

Paterson, David, and Mary Dee Hicks. "Development First," *Personnel Decisions.*

Raskas, Bernard. *Heart of Wisdom, Book 2.* The Burning Book Press, 1979.

Rohrlich, Jay, M.D. *Work and Love.* Summit Books, 1980.

Schmookler, Andrew Bard. *Fools Gold.* Harper, 1993.

Shwartz, Jeffrey. *A Return to Innocence.* Regan Books/HarperCollins, 1998.

Siu, R. G. *The Master Manager.* Mentor Books/New American Library, 1980.

Storr, Anthony. *Solitude.* Ballantine Books, 1988.

Stuart, Ian. *Does God Play Dice?* Basil Blackwell, 1989.

Wharton, Edith. *The Age of Innocence.* Grosset &
   Dunlap, 1920.
White, Theodore H. *America in Search of Itself.*
   Harper & Row, 1982.
Whyte, David. *The Heart Arouser.* Doubleday, 1994
Wilson, Colin. *The Outsider*, J. P. Tarcher, 1956.
Zaleski, Philip (editor). *The Best Spiritual Writing*,
   HarperSanFrancisco, 1998.

BARRIE SANFORD GREIFF, M.D., is currently a consultant to the Harvard University Health Services.

From 1968 to 1984 he was Psychiatrist to the Harvard Business School and in 1970 pioneered the groundbreaking course The Executive Family, which dealt with the relationship between self, family, and work. His subsequent book *Tradeoffs* (1980, New American Library) addressed those issues. He is also the coauthor of *Impact of Job Loss* (1990, American Psychiatric Press) and *Consultation to Industry* (1993, American Psychiatric Press). He has consulted and lectured to a wide range of organizations, including Putnam Investments, IBM, General Foods, PepsiCo., Digital Equipment Corp., AT&T, Corning, Bank-Boston, Toyota, a number of Big Five accounting firms, law firms, and MIT's Sloan School.

Dr. Greiff is a Fellow of the American Psychiatric Association and a Diplomat of the American Board of Psychiatry and Neurology. At present he conducts a private practice in Cambridge, Massachusetts, continues to consult to a number of organizations and is a board member of several companies.

He is married, with three children and two grandchildren.